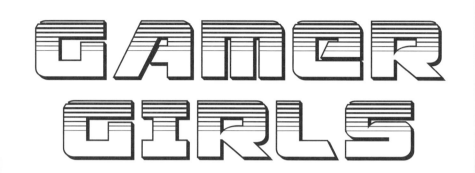

GAMER GIRLS

25 Women Who Built the Video Game Industry

Written by MARY KENNEY

Illustrated by SALINI PERERA

RP|TEENS
PHILADELPHIA

Running Press Teens
Hachette Book Group
1290 Avenue of the Americas, New York, NY 10104
www.runningpress.com/rpkids
@RP_Kids

Printed in China

First Edition: July 2022

Published by Running Press Teens, an imprint of Perseus Books, LLC, a subsidiary of Hachette Book Group, Inc. The Running Press Teens name and logo is a trademark of the Hachette Book Group.

The Hachette Speakers Bureau provides a wide range of authors for speaking events. To find out more, go to www.hachettespeakersbureau.com or call (866) 376-6591.

The publisher is not responsible for websites (or their content) that are not owned by the publisher.

Interior and cover illustrations by Salini Perera
Print book cover and interior design by Marissa Raybuck

Library of Congress Cataloging-in-Publication Data has been applied for.

ISBNs: 978-0-7624-7456-1 (hardcover), 978-0-7624-7455-4 (ebook)

1010

10 9 8 7 6 5 4 3 2 1

To Jason, who didn't stop believing in me,
and to all the women in this book,
who didn't stop believing in themselves.

CONTENTS

INTRODUCTION

I APPROACHED WRITING this book with a simple goal in mind: to show girls that they can make video games. Young girls, teenage girls, middle-aged girls, cis girls, trans girls, Black girls, Asian girls, mixed-race girls, people who aren't girls at all but are reading this book, girls who want to be bosses and girls who don't, girls who love math and girls who love art. Any girl can be a game developer.

Like me. I'm currently a "AAA" developer, which is someone who works on games with blockbuster budgets. I work at Insomniac Games and was a writer on 2020's *Marvel's Spider-Man: Miles Morales* and 2021's *Ratchet & Clank: Rift Apart*. Before that, I was at a smaller but well-known studio called Telltale Games until it closed in 2018. Before and after Telltale, I contributed writing and design to about a dozen games: some announced, some not, some canceled, and some so early in pre-production that I won't even recognize the game when it comes out. So it goes in game development.

My first solo project was a hypertext game about a monster who lived behind the faux wood paneling of a trailer home. That project led to more projects and, suddenly, I was accepted into the master's game design program at New York University. I've been called a game writer, designer, narrative designer, narrative writer, and creative lead. I call myself a writer.

There are a lot of people who want to do what I do, or at least wonder if they want to do what I do. I give as many talks, mentorships, and Q&A sessions as I can to help people figure out if this is their dream job. A few months before I started working on this book, I was asked to speak at a game design boot camp for teenage girls. *Yes!* I thought, *More young women in the games industry!*

I video-conferenced in (they were in the Midwest, and I lived in California at the time). I put on a wide smile and introduced myself. I talked about what a game writer does, which is everything from pitching level ideas to character arcs to writing dialogue. I gave an overview of the production process. I talked about portfolios, skillsets, and going to college. I outlined the importance of teamwork, collaboration, and humility. Then, when I was through with my spiel, I asked if anyone had questions. Hands shot up, and I was thrilled. I couldn't wait to talk more about the industry and projects I love.

Question one: "Could you tell us about Gamergate?"

Followed by: "Has anyone attacked you online?"

Then: "Doesn't the harassment make you want to leave?"

I could feel myself deflate. Is that all they wanted to talk about? Online harassment campaigns and hate mobs?

The purpose of this book is to show that any girl can be a game developer, but as I was writing it, I had to face a simple but devastating question:

"Do I believe it?"

"Yes" is my knee-jerk, stubborn reply. My more measured version is: "Yes, but there are obstacles, often unfair ones." On my worst days, days when I feel strung out, deflated, and gritty with tears, my answer is: "Sometimes."

There are a few things that will reduce me to "sometimes" as quickly as Gamergate and the toxic spaces it left behind. This isn't a book about Gamergate, but in any discussion of modern games and the people who made them, it's impossible to ignore.

Gamergate changed the way people live online and off it, especially in the slice of the world we call the video game industry. Death threats and harassing mobs drove talented developers away from the industry, subjecting underrepresented gamedevs and creatives and those defending them to an avalanche of abuse that still resurfaces. Women and gender non-conforming creators of color in particular were targeted by the attacks but left out of the coverage that followed. At the core of the Gamergate mob was a question about identity: Who was allowed to be a "gamer," and who wasn't? For a small but vocal and aggressive minority, it seemed that if you weren't a white, cis, able-bodied man, you weren't allowed to be part of games—either as a developer or player. As the *Washington Post* wrote in 2014, "Gamergate is less a one-off scandal . . . and more a long-term, slow-burning campaign. In other words, *Gamergate is not going away*." Despite its impact, very few people know how to categorize it, let alone stop it. Game studios have tried. *The New York Times* has tried. The United Nations, countless internet threads, Game Developers Conference talks—they've all tried. The results have been so frustrating that many of us, especially those who have been harassed by "ex-Gamergaters," respond to questions about Gamergate with: "Can we talk about something else?"

So it took me a few moments to respond when the girls asked me about Gamergate. To their credit, they waited for me to collect my thoughts. As silent moments ticked by, I realized I had to tell them *exactly* how I felt about Gamergate. I'd offered them a look at what it meant to be a game developer. That includes the fun things like launch parties, gaming conferences, and announcement trailers, but it also includes one of the cruelest, most defining moments of pop culture in the last twenty years. These girls wanted to make games, but they'd also grown up reading a torrent of articles that chronicled, sometimes in lurid detail, all the toxicity, hate campaigns, and doxing that seemed to come along with the job. If I were them, I'd ask the same thing.

I answered the questions, starting with a brief history of Gamergate. I made it clear that I was not an expert, nor am I now, and that I wasn't even working on games when it happened. Yes, I said, I'd been attacked online, though I'd never been doxed. That left one question, the most devastating: Did Gamergate ever make me want to stop making games?

Certainly, there were days when I wanted to leave social media. But completely leave game development? No, not really, because this is my *dream job*. It can be difficult, like working in any field, but there's so much more happening behind the scenes than what players, even passionate ones, ever see. Days spent perfecting a two-page script, then watching a senior executive cry over it. Forming inside jokes with actors that reduced us all to tears. (Does it sound like there's a lot of crying in video game development? That's because there *is* a lot of crying in video game development.) BUGS, oh, the bugs. Watching players laugh at your jokes, then cry at your favorite scenes, and cheer as they solve a puzzle you spent months building—that's all part of game development, even if you never see it on social media or in press tours.

The women in this book have similar stories. They describe deadlines, launch parties, code patches, being overworked, being demoralized after a lackluster game launch, and finding the will to keep going. Many of them told me stories about their regrets, but also the joys that keep them in this flawed, fragile, thrilling, fast-paced industry. To quote game designer and former NYU Game Center director Frank Lantz, "Making games combines everything that's hard about building a bridge with everything that's hard about composing an opera. Games are operas made out of bridges."

Women aren't new to this industry, though for many years they didn't get as much credit as they deserved. For example, take Kazuko Shibuya, a Japanese video game artist who worked on the original *Final Fantasy* game and created some of the most iconic art in the *Final Fantasy* series. However, despite her vital ideas and work, she wasn't included in the first game's credits, and she didn't even have a Wikipedia page until 2019, when she spoke on a panel at Japan Expo in Paris and drew the attention of gamers and journalists alike. Kazuko went thirty-two years with little to no credit for her work, which is both ridiculous and unfair. Without her—and many like her—the industry wouldn't look the way it does today. Maybe the industry wouldn't even *be here.*

This book is a collection of histories like Kazuko's: stories of the women who loved games enough to make them and whose lives became interwoven with a young, creative, explosive, thrilling business. Who stared at computers and thought, "But what if . . . ?" This book is an answer to the question "Hasn't Gamergate made you want to quit?" and why so many of us say "No." The stories in this book are about passion, hope, resilience, optimism, and grit. I hope, as you read this book, you see all of those qualities in them, and in yourself.

Any girl can be a game developer.

It's easy to say, but do I believe it?

Yes, I think I do.

GLOSSARY

THIS BOOK USES terminology that's common to video games and nowhere else. Or, worse, terms that *are* common, but game developers use them in a totally different way. If a weird word shows up in only one chapter, I'll explain it there. For more common terms, flip to this glossary. You might even want to bookmark it.

AAA (OR TRIPLE-A): Considered the "blockbusters" of video games: budgets of millions of dollars, teams of hundreds of people, and sales goals in the multimillions. "AAA" doesn't refer to a game's quality or genre.

ADVENTURE GAMES: A genre in which the player is the protagonist, the game is an interactive story, and gameplay is exploration, dialogue, and solving puzzles. *Colossal Cave Adventure* was the first adventure game, which inspired Roberta Williams to write the genre-defining *King's Quest* series (her chapter is coming up!).

ASSETS: Things that go in the game. A weapon, a line of dialogue, a piece of furniture: all assets. You'll often hear gamedevs talk about "asset management" or "requesting an asset," which just means "putting stuff in the game."

BOSS FIGHT: A challenging computer-controlled enemy that the player must defeat. If it's the last fight in a game or level, it's called the "final boss." Boss fights test a player's mastery of a game's mechanics, such as fighting with a sword or leaping between platforms. The hardest video game boss? My vote is for the Valkyrie Queen in *God of War* (2018), but I could be talked into Sephiroth in *Kingdom Hearts 2* (2006).

BUGS: Nightmare fuel. A bug is something that goes wrong in a game. Bugs are "fun" because they can happen to any department, at any time, and at any scale. Environments vanish. Characters crumple to the ground in their "death" state for, like, no reason. Dialogue won't play. Some bugs are considered "game breakers," so bad that a player can't keep playing if they run into it. Other bugs are minor or even unnoticeable. Some bugs aren't game breakers, but they're major enough to need solving. For example, when a character's eyes are broken (yikes), and the pupils spin like merry-go-rounds during cutscenes. That won't stop you from playing the game, so it's not a game breaker, but it'll definitely affect how much you're able to pay attention to Creepy-Eyes McGee's dialogue, so it's a top priority.

DAY-ONE PATCH: Software update released the same day a video game goes live. Sometimes, developers "finish" a game knowing that they'll create a "day-one patch" to fix or add things to the game. Maybe the developers ran out of time, or their staff got moved onto a different project. Maybe a bug wasn't spotted until they'd already stopped working on the game. Whatever the reason, the day-one patch is meant to solve the problem. In a few extreme cases, day-one patches have even added or cut major content, such as storylines, quests, mechanics, and characters.

DOWNLOADABLE CONTENT (OR DLC): Stuff added to a game after its initial release date that's not a "fix." Just extra content. Sometimes it's free, sometimes not. It can range from fifteen-hour stories to a single new character or map.

EASTER EGG: Like chocolate-filled goodies hidden in backyards, video game Easter eggs are hidden features or messages. If you want to be really cool at parties, whip out this Game History 101 knowledge: in the 1976 hypertext game *Colossal Cave Adventure*, if you type in the command "XYZZY," it lets you switch spots on the map. Yes, fast travel was the very first Easter egg, though the name "Easter egg" wasn't used until a few years later.

GAME DESIGNER: To oversimplify it, designers are in charge of the player experience. Mmkay . . . what does that mean? Designers lay out levels, create puzzles, and are in charge of the moment-to-moment journey of the player. Creativity and technical know-how are key to being a good game designer.

GAMEDEV: More of a catch-all descriptor than a job title, a game developer, or gamedev, is anyone who works in games. Gamedevs can be writers, animators, artists, quality assurance specialists, you name it.

GAME DEVELOPERS CONFERENCE (OR GDC): A massive, influential, informative, educational, raucous, pain-in-the-neck week that feels a lot like college. Gamedevs—students, amateurs, and pros—gather to talk about goals, past mistakes, genre-bending ideas, and new technologies.

GAME ENGINE: What the game "runs on," like the engine in a car. An engine manages everything from physics to asset management. Some studios and publishers use independent or proprietary engines, meaning engines they built themselves. Others use third-party engines, which are engines another company built, such as Unreal or Unity.

GAMERGATE: For those who lived through it, Gamergate never really went away. It was a harassment campaign that targeted journalists and game developers, focusing on women, Black, Indigenous, Asian, Latinx, and other creators of color, the LGBTQ+ community, and the allies who supported them. It caused a chilling effect in the industry, and we are still recovering from it.

INDIE GAME: There is a ton of discussion and disagreement on what this term actually means, so here's the basic gist: indie, or independent, games are made by teams—or in some cases a single person—who don't work directly for a publisher. Teams tend to be smaller and budgets lower than those of AAA games. *Undertale* (2015), *Hades* (2020), and *Stardew Valley* (2016) are examples of indie games.

LAUNCH DATE/LAUNCH PARTY: The fancy term for "ship date." This is the day the game can be purchased, downloaded, and played. Woo, it's finally out! It's often celebrated with, you guessed it, a giant party.

MECHANICS: What you do in a game to play it. The queen's movement in chess is a mechanic; the ability to walk across a map in *The Elder Scrolls V: Skyrim* is a mechanic. As you can probably imagine, gamedevs talk about mechanics, sometimes called "verbs," a lot.

NON-PLAYER CHARACTER (OR NPC): Any character in the game that isn't controlled by the player. Seriously, that's it. Some have minor roles and show up for only a few sentences. Others are major characters, companions, or even romance options. All of them fall under the NPC umbrella.

PATCH: An update intended to "fix" something in the game after it ships. Sometimes this means fixing a bug (see above definition). Other times, it's a response to player feedback. In rare cases, a patch adds or changes something major, such as a storyline or character, like when BioWare's *Mass Effect: Andromeda* patched in a same-sex romance option.

PERMADEATH: If you die in the game, you die in real life! No, wait, not that. Permadeath, or permanent death, means: if a character dies in the game, they stay dead. This can apply to non-player characters or the player. If it's the former, you say goodbye to them forever. If it's the latter, your options are typically to start over, reload an old save, or cry. Maybe all three.

PUBLISHER: Typically, the company footing the bill for a game's creation, marketing, and distribution. Publishers don't usually make games—studios do that—but some do. Some studios have turned into publishers, such as Atari and Electronic Arts.

RELEASE DATE: The same as a launch or ship date, it's the day a game can be downloaded and played. Announcing it is guaranteed to make any developer sweat. "Huh, guess that's the deadline, no take-backs." Unless it's moved forward or back, which happens.

ROGUELIKE GAMES: A subgenre of role-playing games that a lot of people talk about without really knowing what they are. The most recognizable feature of roguelike games are procedurally generated maps. Roguelikes also typically feature turn-based gameplay and permadeath. A popular roguelike game is *Hades*.

ROLE-PLAYING GAMES (OR RPGS): A genre in which the player assumes the role of a character in a fictional setting. RPGs often feature branching storylines, dialogue mechanics, character stats, and relationship-building with non-player characters. Many game writers got their love of video games from RPGs, including yours truly.

SHIPPABLE: Not the kissing kind. Well, not always. In games, shippable means: good enough for people to play it. Shippable means something is good and ready for launch, not perfect. If you try to make a perfect game, you'll never ship anything. But trying to make a good one? Totally doable. And, yeah, gamedevs ship characters in the kissing way, too (one look at our Twitter feeds can tell you that).

SHIP DATE: The day the game can be downloaded and played, also called a launch or release date. Ship dates can move around a lot depending on production, bugs (they keep coming up, don't they?), staffing, schedules, marketing, and more.

STUDIO: A company or group that makes video games. Sometimes a studio is one developer. Sometimes they employ thousands. A studio employs the people creating the game: writers, designers, lighting artists, dialogue engineers, and more. Studios often answer to publishers (see definition above) or even turn into publishers.

VERTICAL SLICE: A piece of the game, such as a level or map, that's created early (sometimes first!) in a game's production. It's intended to show what the game will look and feel like when it's finished. After making a slice, designers and creatives make big decisions, like what to scrap, what to keep working on, and what is special about their game.

ROBERTA WILLIAMS

The storyteller who asked,
"What if you could play them?"

WHITE, BULKY SQUARE blinks at you, waiting for your input. Above it, just a few words: "Welcome to Adventure!! Would you like instructions?" You type "yes," and a wall of text appears, inviting you to explore the Colossal Cave. But be warned: many adventurers who venture into its depths don't come back. *Colossal Cave Adventure* is a text game about an elaborate cave system, but when Roberta Williams first played it, she wasn't thinking about how to survive. She was thinking about writing a game of her own.

The Greatest Imagination

More than twenty years before Roberta ever wrote or even played a video game, she was born in La Verne, a small city about thirty miles east of Los Angeles. She wasn't submersed in technology or early computers as a child, as many game designers are. The year was 1953, and her father was a horticulturist, someone who studies and cultivates plants and gardens. Her mother was a painter and housewife. She didn't have video games or a laptop, but Roberta had books and a vivid imagination. She loved to write stories and plays, and she had "characters in her head" from the time she was small.

Roberta met Ken, her future husband, when she was still in high school. They married when she was nineteen years old and had their first son a year later. Her second son was born six years after that, in 1979, the same year she played *Colossal Cave Adventure* for the first time.

Roberta never went to college, but she describes her education as "lots and lots of Fairy Tales, [and] the greatest imagination of the 20th century." No arguments here: within a few years of playing *Colossal Cave Adventure*, she'd become one of the twentieth century's most influential game writers and designers. But in 1979, the technology to create her stories didn't exist—because she and her husband hadn't invented it yet.

Putting the Graphic in Adventure

Roberta and Ken were out to dinner one night when she decided to tell him her idea: she wanted to write an interactive murder mystery that could be played on a computer. At the time, Ken was working on a compiler, a program that translates computer languages, but Roberta persuaded him to work on her idea instead. She would write, design, and illustrate the game if he would program it. He agreed, and, just like that, *Mystery House* was officially in development.

The game's first challenge? Illustrations. Games on home computers didn't have graphics back then, but Roberta wanted graphics, not just text, for the player to interact with as they tried to solve the murder mystery. If you've ever played a text adventure, you probably understand why: half of your mind is trying to imagine the game's levels and maps, and the other half is actually trying to play it. Roberta wanted players to focus on the story, and to do that, she had to build the levels and maps for them.

But the technology to create the graphics Roberta wanted didn't exist yet, so Ken and Roberta *invented* it. It happened in two parts: Roberta bought a VersaWriter, a machine that might as well be a unicorn, because it's almost impossible to find anymore. The VersaWriter is a white plastic "drawing board" with a mechanical arm that's used to trace pictures that could be read by the Apple II computer. Roberta drew the pictures she wanted for *Mystery House* on the VersaWriter, but its software couldn't handle pictures more complex than graphs or floor plans. That's where Ken came in: he created more complex software so the Apple II and VersaWriter could handle Roberta's drawings. Adventure game graphics were born.

A Cabin in the Woods

Ten thousand copies. That was the number Roberta and Ken needed to sell to live in their dream house, a cabin in rural California. If they sold more than 10,000 copies, they could even think about making games full-time. That was a stretch, but not impossible. Roberta's idea might make all their dreams come true.

Roberta and Ken knew their audience was limited: few people owned home computers in the 1980s, mainly programmers and engineers. Still, Roberta hoped her murder mystery would appeal to people who had no coding background, just as *Colossal Cave Adventure* had appealed to her. So, she wrote the game's core mechanic, typed-in commands, to be simple and obvious to people without experience in programming, such as "open door" and "up stairs."

In May 1980, Roberta and Ken took out an advertisement in *MICRO: The 6502 Journal*, a magazine for the techiest of tech people. "TIRED OF BUYING GAMES THAT BECOME BORING AFTER A FEW HOURS OF PLAY?" the ad began. "An adventure game is a fantasy world where you are transported, via your own computer. . . . You are transported to the front yard of a large, old Victorian home. When you enter the house, you are pulled into the mystery, murder, and intrigue and cannot leave until you solve the puzzles. Your friends are being murdered one by one. You must find out why, and who the killer is. Be careful, because the killer may find you!"

Ten thousand copies. The ad, the mechanics, and the graphics just needed to get them 10,000 copies.

Three months after *Mystery House* shipped, Roberta and Ken had sold enough copies to move away from Los Angeles and build their cabin in the woods.

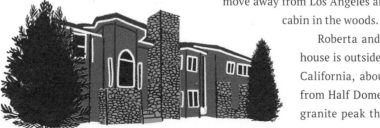

Roberta and Ken's dream house is outside of Oakhurst, California, about fifty miles from Half Dome, the smooth granite peak that dominates

Yosemite National Park. Today, the house is a testament to everything Roberta and Ken built together. On either side of the front door are stained-glass windows, that depict characters from the 1982 movie *The Dark Crystal*, which Roberta and Ken adapted into a video game in 1983. There is even an Apple logo painted on the floor of the indoor basketball court. And in one of the bathrooms, there is a circular stained-glass window that depicts a mountain peak ringed by rich blue, the logo of the company Roberta and Ken founded together: Sierra On-Line.

SIDE QUEST — ANNE WESTFALL

The 1982 game *Tax Dodge* might be the *only* action game ever made about avoiding taxes, and it was because programmer Anne Westfall and her husband wanted to make a violence-free game. A year after *Tax Dodge* debuted, they shipped what's probably their best-known game, *Archon: The Light and the Dark*. Anne handled the bulk of the programming for the first and second *Archon* games, which were among the first published by a then little-known company called Electronic Arts. Before she became a video game programmer, Anne was a software engineer. She was responsible for designing the first microcomputer-based program that could lay out housing subdivisions. Sounds like a good foundation (ha! sorry, couldn't resist) for a video game level designer, doesn't it?

Sierra Comes On-Line

Roberta and Ken had sold more than enough copies of *Mystery House* to move and build their dream house, but now they had a different problem: boxes, stacks and stacks of them. The Williamses were inundated with fan mail and orders. To try to keep up, they hired a few employees, but the boxes kept stacking up. And the phone wouldn't stop ringing. Roberta put her foot down at Ken's idea to hire someone to answer her own home phone (cell phones weren't a thing yet). It was time to get an office.

Sierra On-Line's office opened in Oakhurst, eventually employing one thousand people in a town of seven thousand. Over the next decade, Sierra became one of the most well-known video game companies in the world. Three months after *Mystery House*, Roberta and Ken released *The Wizard and the Princess*, a game that added color to the still-new concept of graphics. Sierra On-Line released three more games in the next three years—a rapid-fire pace for any writer, and an unbelievable one for a game designer. Roberta wrote many of these titles, but as the company grew, other writers added to the catalogue. Chuck Benton wrote *Softcore Adventure*, which led to *Leisure Suit Larry*. Jane Jensen (her chapter starts on page 117) wrote the *Gabriel Knight* series. Sierra had become the undisputed leader of adventure games, but it was the game Roberta wrote four years after *Mystery House* that most people remember her for—a little game called *King's Quest*.

The game begins with the dying King Edward sending a young knight, Graham—that's you, the player—on a quest to destroy a wicked witch and find three treasures. The game combined a fantasy setting with exploration, problem solving, and humor, and gamers loved it. The game skyrocketed, launching seven sequels and by 1997, the series had sold more than 7 million copies.

King's Quest was huge for Roberta and Sierra On-Line, but it also presented a problem: Roberta was afraid she would be "typecast" as someone who wrote only fun, family-friendly games, and she wanted to do more. She wanted to keep pushing Sierra's technology and tell a very different kind of story—one she'd started writing and stopped several times before she finally committed to seeing it through: a horror game.

Everyone's Got a Favorite

Some people compare making games to having kids: they're all different, and it's impossible to pick your favorite. Not for Roberta. *Phantasmagoria* (1995) is her favorite, and it's unlike anything Roberta made before or since.

Phantasmagoria is the story of Adrienne Delaney, played by actress Victoria Morsell, who moves into a remote mansion with her husband, Don. As she settles into the house, supernatural forces begin to play with her mind. As the player, you must help Adrienne uncover the secrets of the mansion before it destroys her. The premise, a haunted mansion, might sound similar to *Mystery House*, but the overall tone is much different. *Mystery House* was a brain-bending murder mystery. *Phantasmagoria*? Grim, dark horror.

When Roberta was just four years old, she watched the movie *Horrors of the Black Museum* (1959) and was so disturbed by it, she swore off horror films altogether. At least, until she was a teenager. Movies like *Halloween* (1978), *Carrie* (1976), and *The Shining* (1980) drew her back into the genre, and after the success of *Mystery House* and founding of Sierra, she wanted to write something scary. Before writing *Phantasmagoria*'s screenplay—yes, she did write it, in the style of a movie—Roberta spent six months watching horror movies, reading thriller novels, and asking friends to tell her every scary story they knew. Stephen King and Edgar Allan Poe were among her influences.

Roberta designed it as a point-and-click adventure set in a spooky mansion, like *Mystery House*, but otherwise, *Phantasmagoria* would be different from anything else Roberta had made. While other Sierra games were graphics only, Roberta wanted *Phantasmagoria* to incorporate full-motion video, or FMV, which means recordings of live actors would play in the game. Roberta also wanted the game to be shot and scored like a movie—which meant Sierra would need to invest in technology no one had used in games before.

The initial screenplay clocked in at 550 pages, roughly five times the length of a traditional Hollywood screenplay. Roberta wrote eight hundred scenes, which would take two hundred people two years to develop, with an extra four months to film. Though that's a normal amount of time to spend making a game these days, at the time, Sierra typically took around a year to make a game.

Roberta spared no expense to bring her vision of *Phantasmagoria* to life, either. Sierra built a $1.5 million blue-screen (the predecessor to green screens) studio to film live actors, and they hired a Hollywood special effects studio as well. Those investments added up. The budget for the game was $800,000, but it ended up costing $4.5 million, not including the new blue-screen studio. *Phantasmagoria* needed to sell well to make that money back, but no one was sure it would. It wasn't anything like *King's Quest* and was much darker than *Mystery House*. Even Ken, who was always supportive of Roberta's work, worried about *Phantasmagoria*. He feared it was too violent, too expensive, and too focused on combat-free gameplay to be successful. If it didn't sell well, *Phantasmagoria* would go down as one of the biggest financial flops in video game history.

Thankfully, it didn't. All the things Ken had worried about were what made *Phantasmagoria* stand out from its competition. Players loved the mystery, the live actors, and the horror, and they were more than happy to buy and install all seven CD-ROMs' worth of data to play it. It made $12 million in its first weekend, selling 300,000 copies, and went on to become Sierra's best-selling computer game of all time.

On Sierra's Shoulders

The year was 2014, thirty-five years after Roberta first played *Colossal Cave Adventure*. The place was The Game Awards, one of the biggest awards shows for video games. Neil Druckmann, creative director of *The Last of Us* and *Uncharted 4: A Thief's End*, stood behind a silver podium preparing to give out one of the most coveted honors that can be given to any gamedev: the Industry Icon Award.

Neil opened his speech with his own memories of Sierra. "Growing up in Israel, I barely knew any English," Neil said. "But I pored through Sierra's catalogue bit by bit, sitting there with a Hebrew-English dictionary. I learned to read and write English so I could play every *King's Quest*, every *Space Quest*, and, when my parents weren't around, *Leisure Suit Larry*." The audience laughed, and Neil continued, "Today's gaming storytellers stand on Sierra's shoulders."

The screens at the back of the stage parted, and Roberta and Ken walked out. Neil presented them with the award, and the audience cheered as Roberta shook Neil's hand. Ken gave a speech while Roberta waved to the crowd. "Almost to the day, thirty-five years ago, that I was playing an adventure game that was all text on a teletype machine . . . and Roberta saw me playing it, and kind of took over the screen. A few days later, she said, we've gotta go to dinner, and she took me to dinner and spent the evening describing her vision for what a game could be." The beginnings of *Mystery House*, and the start of the adventure game genre as we know it.

After Ken wrapped up his part of the speech, he adjusted the microphone to Roberta's height. "I'm a shortie, you know," she opened, and the crowd laughed. She thanked everyone and said she was surprised to be there. She'd been retired for more than a decade by then, but her legacy endured: she introduced the creators of the next *King's Quest* title, drawing more cheers from the crowd.

Ken and Roberta sold Sierra On-Line in 1996, and Roberta's final *King's Quest* game—and final game, period—shipped in 1999. Until 2021, that is, when Ken and Roberta announced they were working on their first game in more than twenty years: *The Secret*. Ken told gaming website *Gamasutra* that he'd been playing with the Unity engine around the time Roberta had a new idea for a game, and just like that, they were back in the game-making business.

What Roberta brought to the video game industry was a love of storytelling and a passionate desire to build the technology to match her narrative goals. Graphics, color, and live actors became part of video games because of Roberta. She may have stepped out of the spotlight for a short time—until she re-entered it in 2021—but her influence never will.

MURIEL TRAMIS

The chevalier of video games

A FIGURE CROUCHES ON a brown and black field. They rise and tear apart shackles binding their wrists as the word "FREEDOM" burns above them. In the 1988 game *Freedom: Rebels in the Darkness*, you play as a slave on a sugar plantation, and you must incite your fellow slaves to revolt. The price of failure is your life. The game's creator calls it a story of "true warriors," much like the creator—a Chevalier of the Legion of Honour—herself.

But I'm getting ahead of the story. Before Muriel Tramis was a chevalier, an engineer, or the first Black woman to design video games, she was a little girl on an island in the Caribbean, a setting she would return to many times in a career of challenging the status quo.

The Island Where It All Began

There is nowhere in the world that hasn't been affected, in one way or another, by colonialism, the spread and domination of one culture over another. An example of colonialism is this book, which was written in North America by someone speaking English rather than one of the many languages of the Indigenous peoples of this area. Martinique, Muriel's place of birth, is no exception. It's there in the name, which is French, even though the island lies in the heart of the Caribbean, as is the national language, though Martinican Creole is just as common to hear. It is easy to see why Muriel, who was born in Martinique, returned to the theme of colonialism several times over the course of her career.

Muriel was born in Martinique in 1958 and grew up in Fort-de-France, the seaside capital marked by brightly painted buildings and encircled by green mountains. As a little girl, Muriel loved to tell stories and create giant live-action role-playing games. She went to school in a convent—yes, the kind with nuns—and when she turned sixteen years old, she left home to study engineering in Paris, France.

Muriel graduated from the Institut Supérieur d'Electronique de Paris in the early 1980s, one of seven women in a class of seventy. She started her career in the weapons industry, making unmanned aerial vehicles and remotely piloted aircrafts smarter by improving their artificial intelligence. But after five years, Muriel started to feel conflicted about her work. Elijah Lee, writing for *The Icon*, asked Muriel what it was about her job that drove her away: Was it a moral objection to weapons and war, or had she lost interest? "Well, it was both actually," she told him. "It was already a moral question, because I was around arms dealers whose mentality I didn't like at all. Secondly, I did not find this field of work creative enough, though really I hadn't realized it at the time. It was afterwards, in retrospect, that I realized I wanted to create my own material, and not program things I was forced to do."

Muriel decided to leave engineering altogether and pursue something more creative—but not games. First, she decided to study marketing. That led to an internship at a company that sold educational games. Through that job, she learned about a studio called Coktel Vision, which made educational and adventure games. Muriel interned with Coktel, and near the end of her internship, she decided to pitch her first video game: *Méwilo*.

"The Roberta Williams of France"

Later in her career, Muriel would become known as the French Roberta Williams because they shared a passion for storytelling and interesting design. Muriel's first game was no exception. *Méwilo* is a story about racism, the paranormal, and colonial history, inspired by the Carib legend about jars of gold. The legend goes that during the revolts of the 1800s and early 1900s, plantation owners hid their gold by ordering enslaved people to hide it in jars. After they buried the jars, the owners killed them and buried them alongside the gold, hoping their restless ghosts would protect their wealth from thieves. In *Méwilo*, you play a paranormal expert visiting friends in Saint-Pierre, Martinique, and you discover that something is haunting their house. As you investigate, you confront Martinique's history of racism and rebellion. The game's final twist ties into Martinique's real history, a natural disaster that changed the island forever.

To turn the legend into a game, Muriel asked her friend, Patrick Chamoiseau, to help with the story. Patrick, a Black writer from Martinique, was part of the *créolité* literary movement that began with Martinican writers, described as "an annihilation of false universality, of monolinguism, and of purity" in the French Caribbean. He would go on to create everything from books to comics to theater.

The game is steeped in its Martinican influences, from its setting to the bonus gifts that came with the game: a short story written by Patrick, a recipe for the Creole vegetable dish callaloo, and a cassette tape featuring songs from Malavoi, a Martinican band. For all of these reasons, the city of Paris awarded *Méwilo* a silver medal for historical and cultural significance.

Muriel's next game, *Freedom: Rebels in the Darkness*, was similarly inspired by Martinique's history. You play as one of four enslaved Black people, each with different skills, trying to start a rebellion on an eighteenth-century French plantation. The strategy game, also co-created with Patrick Chamoiseau, is both riveting and devastating to play. You sneak through the night, avoiding watchdogs and guards who could hurt or kill you, hoping to persuade the others to join your rebellion. You befriend either a medicine man or a shaman, the only ones who can heal your wounds. Each time you ask someone to help you, the answer is randomized, either "yes" or "no," so every interaction has an equal chance of failing. If you persuade enough people to rebel, you fight for your freedom.

"Fugitive slaves, my ancestors, were true warriors that I had to pay tribute to," Muriel told *Wired* magazine in 2010. "At the time I made the game, these stories were not known. It was my duty to remember."

ELIZABETH LAPENSÉE

Elizabeth Lapensée was one of the first game designers to center Indigenous cultures and experiences in her work. Her 2014 board game *The Gift of Food* featured Northwest Native foods. Five years later, she shipped *When Rivers Were Trails*, a video game about the displacement of the Anishinaabe peoples in Canada and the United States in the 1890s. *When Rivers Were Trails* won the 2019 IndieCade Adaptation Award, given to a game that's a reimagined real-world event or other piece of media. Along with her work designing games, Elizabeth has a PhD, teaches at Michigan State, and writes comics.

"France Loves Stories"

To make a video game, you have to convince other people that your idea is a good one. This is usually called a pitch: you're pitching the idea of a game to other developers or a publisher, and they decide whether they want to work on or pay for it. Making people believe in your idea, whether that idea is to teach history or join a literary movement, is never easy, but Muriel did it over and over again at Coktel Vision. "Back then, the adventure game was king," Muriel told *Wired*. "There were many more scenarios with literary rich universes and characters. There was a ferment of ideas and lots of originality. France loves stories." Muriel explored eroticism in her 1989 game *Emmanuelle*, 1990's *Geisha*, and 1991's *Fascination*, and she created lighthearted romps with 1991's *Gobliiins* and its sequels. She taught kids to enjoy learning with *Adibou* and *La Bosse des maths*. She told stories in multiple genres and styles, and France loved them all.

Then Roberta Williams's career impacted Muriel's in another, more direct way. Sierra On-Line purchased Coktel Vision in 1993. "The Roberta Williams of France" now worked, albeit indirectly, for the actual Roberta Williams. Muriel stayed with the company despite the change in ownership, team size, and budgets. It was all bigger, and Muriel's audience was now worldwide. Still, Coktel's goal remained the same: tell great stories.

When Roberta and Ken Williams sold Sierra On-Line in 1996, Coktel went with it, where it eventually wound up in the hands of Vivendi. This time, Muriel didn't keep faith in the new management or direction. "No more freedom," Muriel told *The Obscuritory* in 2018. "Profitability first, less risky decisions." Muriel left Coktel in 2003 and stopped making games not long after.

The same year that she left Coktel, Muriel founded a company called Avantilles, which creates 3D models that help with city planning, architecture, and even archeology. She reconstructed the Saint-Pierre she had described in *Méwilo* and became engrossed with the

3D modeling and art technologies being used in film. She wrote two novels: *Au coeur du giraumon*, which is semi-autobiographical, and *Contes créoles et cruels*, which is based on Martinican legends.

For more than a decade, it seemed that Muriel had left games behind for good. That is, until 2018, when *Méwilo* turned thirty years old. Muriel and three other game developers launched an online campaign to fund a remake that would feature "a new adventure based on the first point & click adventure video game." Unfortunately, the campaign raised just under 5,000 euros, less than 10 percent of its €50,000 goal. In April 2018, the developers shut down the crowdfunding project. *Méwilo* had launched Muriel's career and brand as a game designer, but it wasn't ready for a revival.

The Chevalier of Games

Paris Games Week is one of the largest trade shows for video games in the world, right next to E3, Gamescom, and the Tokyo Game Show. The same year the *Méwilo* remake was shelved, Muriel was invited to the show—but not just as a speaker or panelist. She was there for an even higher honor. Mounir Mahjoubi, the French secretary of state at the time, named Muriel Tramis a Chevalier of the Legion of Honour. The Legion of Honour is France's highest order of merit, both for civilians and military, and it is given to recognize exceptional service to France. Muriel was chosen for her contributions to the French video game industry and cultural examinations that focused on Martinique. She was the second game designer to be awarded the honor.

Muriel became history because she was willing to write about it: its ugliness and beauty, its harshness and possibility. Her fearlessness was that of a warrior, not unlike the true warriors she worked so hard to honor.

KARLA ZIMONJA

By all logic, *Gone Home* should have failed. The game was the brain child of a team of veteran developers and Karla Zimonja was one of them. She started in games as an animator before cofounding Fullbright, where she worked as an editor, 2D artist, researcher, and sometimes-writer. The Fullbright devs wanted to make a video game with no guns, weapons, superpowers, health bars, sanity meters, inventory systems, or enemies. So what was left? *Gone Home*, a game that came to define an *entire* genre. The walking simulator is the story of a family told through the things they've left behind in an empty house. Not only was its gameplay noteworthy and its storytelling unique, but it was also one of the first games to feature a lesbian main character. The game has sold more than 700,000 copies since its release in 2013 and has won scores of awards. A year after *Gone Home* shipped, a journalist asked Karla her thoughts on Gamergate. "Steve [her cofounder] doesn't have an agenda," she said. "I have a f***ing agenda. I want to help even out some of the inequality."

DONA BAILEY

The arachnophobe who gave us pastels

T HE YEAR? 1980. The games? Arcade. The hair? Huge. The music? "Space Invader" by the Pretenders. Yes, technically it released in 1979, but people were listening to it in the 1980s, so it still counts. Entirely instrumental, the rock/punk/hip-hop guitar is interspliced with sound effects from, you guessed it, the arcade game *Space Invaders*. During the last ten seconds of the song, as the guitars and drums fade away, you can hear the *pew-pew-pew* and tinny explosions of the shoot-the-aliens arcade game.

And that's how Dona Bailey got into games.

Dona, then a programmer at General Motors, heard the song, but she couldn't figure out what it was about. It had no lyrics, lots of weird sounds, and, as far as she could tell, nothing to do with either space or invaders. So a friend offered to take her to lunch and show her what was so *Space Invader*-y about it. He took her to a "crummy bar" (Dona's words) with one very important feature: an arcade cabinet. "He gave me a quarter, and I lost all my lives before I could even figure out what I was supposed to do on the screen," Dona told the Associated Press in 2012. "But I got really intrigued."

It's easy to envision Dona's hand on the left-right buttons as she tried to stop the aliens from invading. "And I remember standing there thinking, 'God, this looks a lot like what I do.'" Questions flooded her mind: Who made *Space Invaders*, and where were their offices? Were there other arcade cabinets like this one? How many?

And crucially: Could she make something like this?

Dona thought the display and microprocessor in the arcade cabinet looked *a lot* like what she coded on a daily basis. She figured if she could program Cadillacs, there was a good chance she could program games. Dona asked around and learned that Atari was located in Sunnyvale, California. She didn't wait to learn more: she quit her job, packed her bags, and moved north. It was time to get a job making video games.

Constant Change

Dona was born in Little Rock, Arkansas, in 1955. During Dona's childhood, the city grew to a population of more than 100,000; three major television stations began broadcasting; and when Dona was a toddler, nine Black students enrolled in a formerly all-white high school and became known as the Little Rock Nine. Cities, technology, and society were all changing.

One of those things was Dona. Although she loved school growing up, by the time she reached high school, Dona was bored. After 11th grade, she couldn't stand the idea of coming back for another year of high school. So, at sixteen years old, she enrolled in summer classes at The University of Arkansas at Little Rock. She stuck around for the fall semester and just never left.

Three years later, Dona graduated and enrolled in Memphis State's master's program in statistics. She'd always liked school, math, and learning in general, so it surprised her how little she enjoyed the program. She dropped out of Memphis State—"so awkwardly! Bad breakup"—and went back to Little Rock.

Dona was twenty-two years old when she was hired by General Motors in Santa Barbara. She'd worked at the University of Arkansas and had some programming experience, so GM planned to train her in everything else she needed to know. Her "patient coworkers," as she calls them, taught her 6502 assembly language programming, which—little did she know at the time—was the same language being used by early game designers.

"I Wanted to Make a Game That Was Beautiful"

Drawn to games by a song and a cabinet, Dona, now a newly minted Atari programmer, thumbed through a notebook filled with ideas from Atari brainstorming sessions. There were thirty ideas in the little book, and she noticed a trend: sports, guns, tanks, lasers, and explosions. Unfortunately, none of that was particularly interesting to her—except one idea. It was just a single sentence that read: "A multi-segmented insect appears on the screen and is shot by the player from below." Yes, it also had a gun, but Dona figured "it didn't seem that bad to shoot a bug."

When Dona joined Atari in 1980, they didn't have much of a training program for new gamedevs. In Dona's words, it amounted to, "Here's your cubicle, now make your game." She had joined the coin-op division, the department that made the types of arcade games you've probably seen in movies from the 1980s: you stick a coin into a cabinet and bam, you're playing a game. During her first few weeks, Dona had very little idea what she should be doing, and no one seemed all that eager to teach her. Owen Rubin, another programmer in Atari's early days, was the only one who took the time to show her "a million things," and she said later that trying to learn game development on the job was like "shooting blind."

Dona soon learned that programmers at Atari had a range of responsibilities, like creating in-game objects, later called "sprites," animating them, and hand-writing their code. Yes, you read that right: *hand-written*. All the game's coding and graphics were created with some paper and a pencil, and then were fed by someone else into machines called compilers. Dona had to learn all of this without lengthy game engine tutorials, classes, or college majors in game development— just her own smarts and Owen's help.

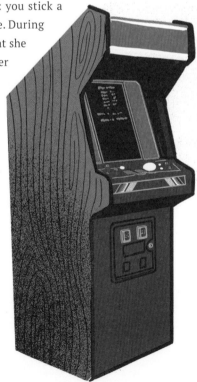

In those days, coin-op games were made by a team ranging from one to four people compared to the teams of dozens, if not hundreds, of people who work on blockbuster games today. If a programmer could create the entire game alone, they did, though this was pretty rare: it was easier and more efficient to divvy up the work with other engineers and technicians than to have to hook up everything yourself. Otherwise, the programmer created as much as she could, the project leader gave ideas and direction, and the game technician and hardware engineer made the hardware work. Since Dona was *Centipede*'s programmer, her personality and preferences were baked into every part of the game's feel, look, and design.

In the game, a centipede winds its way through a maze of mushrooms, and the player's goal is to shoot the mushrooms, or around them, to hit the centipede. The player needs to blast away all segments of the centipede's body before it can reach the bottom of the screen—and you. But then there's the itsy-bitsy spider, which hops all over the screen and exists to make the player's life just a smidge harder. In case you were wondering, we have Dona to thank for the spider, and, likely, for the other enemies introduced alongside it: scorpions and fleas. "[*Centipede*] came out, sort of, because I don't like spiders," she said. "And the spider in that is very cartoonish, and very mischievous, and just irritating, really. And I liked having my way over a spider." *Pew-pew!* Take that, spider.

Apart from the spider, Dona created a crucial element that separated *Centipede* from its competitors: its color palette. "My primary goal," she wrote on a Reddit AMA (ask-me-anything) in 2017, "was to make a game that would be visually appealing to me. I wanted to make a game that was beautiful." At the time, games' color palettes were bold, loud, and bright. The vivid yellows and reds screamed, "COME PLAY ME. I AM VERY COOL. DROP YOUR COINS HERE." And it's not hard to imagine why developers chose bright primary colors. Arcade games were confined to bulky black cases tethered to the wall with power cords and needed to draw attention. *Centipede*, however, broke this unspoken rule, and it drew even more attention because it didn't look like anything else on the market.

Even so, the color scheme's creation was, at least in part, an accident. While a technician was tweaking the arcade machine's hardware, Dona was watching as the display changed. When the technician began, *Centipede* had the usual color spread of primary colors: saturated red, yellow, and blue. Then he tweaked something, and all the colors changed to hot, vivid pastels like neon teal and bright pink. "I made a yip of approval and asked the technician to keep those colors." Yes, it was a bug (pun completely intended) that gave *Centipede* its signature color scheme. "I always thought it was really beautiful," Bailey said of her titular centipede. "Like a shimmering jewel when you walked into the arcade."

In 1981, *Centipede* debuted in bars and arcades across America. The year before, Dona was losing all of her lives in *Space Invaders*, and now she was the programmer behind one of its most popular competitors. *Centipede* quickly became one of the most financially successful games during the "golden era of arcade games" and a big reason for its success was its appeal to women gamers. According to the 1982 book *How To Win Video Games*, competitors like *Defender* had a player base that was only about 5 percent women, while *Centipede*'s was closer to 50 percent. Dona says this was because *Centipede* was designed to be easy to pick up even if you'd never played an arcade game before.

The game began its life with a bunch of buttons, which Dona didn't enjoy at all, so a manager suggested she try a joystick, which was better, but she still didn't love it. Then he suggested a mini trackball, and suddenly it all clicked. "That turned out to be the controller that anyone can walk up to and enjoy using without a learning curve," Dona said. "It was beautiful from the beginning! I loved it, and I was certain anyone else would love it, too."

WENDI ALLEN

Wendi Allen was just a teenager when she started building radios and amplifiers in her spare time. She'd grown up around electronics and loved science: a perfect beginning for one of the most influential hardware engineers in video games. In fact, the art style and vector graphics that defined Atari's early arcade games existed because of Wendi. She created the vector generator display system in *Lunar Lander* and *Asteroids*. The system she created was adapted and later used in nine more Atari games, and Wendi also developed hardware for games like *Superbug*, *Canyon Bomber*, *Firetruck*, and *Smokey Joe*. In 1982, she and many other "ex-Atari" people cofounded Videa, a consulting firm, and Wendi led the coin-op and consumer video game markets division. She is currently self-employed and continues to design all sorts of hardware, from joysticks to photo booths, for a long list of clients, including Capcom and the United States Navy.

Loud Game, Quiet Voice

Outside the walls of Atari HQ, things were going well for Dona. She was the credited programmer on one of the most popular arcade games of all time, and people in the industry knew her name. Inside the walls, however, things weren't going as well for her. At the time, Atari encouraged developers to go on weekend retreats or gather around a conference table to hash out ideas. This meant that, somewhat predictably, extroverts got the advantage. The loudest voices in the room tend to overpower the quieter ones. Dona, always shy, clammed up when pushed to participate. Simultaneously, one of her collaborators on *Centipede* bullied Dona, making her contributions seem less worthwhile than they were.

"It led to a bunch of loud guys saying, 'She has no ideas. She never says anything when we brainstorm,'" Bailey said at the 2007 Women in Games International conference. In that environment, it became difficult for Dona to trust herself, so she left Atari in 1982, a year after *Centipede* debuted. "When I left Atari, I wanted to be able to hear myself think again," she said. "I felt I had lost the ability to always hear the guiding voice in my head due to months of nonstop anger and conflict, both all around me at all times, as well as inside me at all times." Dona had done everything she'd set out to do: create a successful arcade game like the one she'd played in a crummy bar. Now it was time to move on.

Never Lose Curiosity

After working at places like Videa and Activision, Dona left game development in 1985 and moved back to Arkansas. Even then, she didn't completely abandon the industry. She's spoken at conferences, hosted Reddit AMAs, and given interviews to young women trying to become game developers. She's worked on screenplays about her experiences. She also taught at the college level for fifteen years and earned two master's degrees. She inspired hundreds of women, including me, to take their seat at the conference table, even when it's not easy to speak up. "I'm so pleased that there's any possibility that I can be helpful at this point," Dona told *Gamasutra* writer Leigh Alexander in 2007. "I love teaching, because I'm really determined to give back. . . . I've had such a great life, and such a great career, and when I came back to Arkansas and saw that people here really struggle to get an education, it's not something that can be taken for granted."

Never lose curiosity is what Dona tells aspiring game developers over and over again. Never stop learning new skills. Whether it's choosing a new career because of a song, or leaving a career to reconnect with yourself, never lose the sound of your inner voice, and never lose your curiosity.

KAZUKO SHIBUYA

The artist behind the fantasy

W HAT HAPPENS WHEN you land your dream job only to realize that it isn't really want you want to do for the rest of your life? If you're Kazuko Shibuya, you leave that job to find a new one, and along the way help define the art and animation of one of the most important games of all time: *Final Fantasy*.

The Hobby That Became a Dream

Important aside: All interviews with Kazuko were originally done in Japanese and have been translated into English. Since language is weird, translations may not match up perfectly with everything expressed in the original language. Keep in mind that the translator is often trying to capture Kazuko's intent rather than produce a perfect translation. Okay, aside over.

Kazuko was born in 1965, just three years after the first video game, *Spacewar!*, launched on the DEC PDP-1 minicomputer. Video games weren't part of her life growing up, but anime was. In middle school, she spent her spare time doodling illustrations and animations from her favorite anime, *Space Battleship Yamato* and *Galaxy Express 999*. As a teenager, she enrolled in a technical school and worked part-time in a studio, where she got to work on anime like *Area 88*, *Transformers*, and *Obake no Q-taro*. It was a great opportunity, but she didn't find the day-to-day work of an animator fun. She told one of her professors that she wasn't sure whether she wanted to be an animator anymore. Then, in 1986, a game studio looking to improve its art and animation reached out to her. The company's name was Square, and Kazuko's life changed.

When Kazuko joined Square, it wasn't the behemoth publisher known today as Square Enix. It was a much smaller studio focused on making games. Kazuko was twenty-one years old, and she wasn't a gamer; she hadn't played anything Square made. Her family might have owned a Nintendo Famicom, but even if they did, she couldn't remember playing with it. "Even today," she said, in a 2013 interview with *4gamer*, "I don't play games at all." Even so, she decided to take the job, and a year later, Square began work on one of the longest-lasting, most influential, most beloved series in gaming. The project's name was *FF*, at the time, and later it was named *Final Fantasy*.

"Those Days Definitely Seemed Like End Times"

There is a legend about *Final Fantasy* that's so ubiquitous among gamer and pop culture communities, I learned it as a fact in graduate school. The story goes that in the mid-1980s, Square was on the verge of financial disaster and about to close its doors forever. The belea-guered gamedevs at Square pitched one final game, their last mark on the industry before they lost everything. They named it *Final Fantasy* because it was the last game Square would ever make. Then, in a fortuitous twist, the game was so wildly successful and beloved that it singlehandedly saved Square and all of the developers' careers. It's a great story, but it's not true.

In 2015, Hironobu Sakaguchi, the gamedev credited with the creation of the first *Final Fantasy* game, cleared up the rumor-turned-legend while speaking at the Replaying Japan conference in Kyoto. The real reason for *Final Fantasy*'s name is this: The team wanted to name the game something that would abbreviate to "FF," because it sounds good in Japanese. "Fantasy" was the obvious pick for one of those f-words, since they were making a fantasy game. The other word took a little longer to nail down. *Fighting Fantasy* was the first title, but a series of role-playing books already had that name, so that wouldn't work. The team eventually settled on the title we know and love today, *Final Fantasy*.

That's not to say every part of the legend is untrue. "Those days definitely seemed like end times," Sakaguchi said at the conference. Square had made more than twenty games by then, including *The Death Trap* and *King's Knight*. Though *The Death Trap* and its sequel sold more than 100,000 copies, none of Square's other games were runaway hits, and bankruptcy loomed as a real possibility.

Very few people at Square liked the idea of creating a fantasy RPG. They didn't think it would sell well. Kazuko was one of the ones who wasn't sure it would do well, but even so, she offered to help and joined the *FF* team as a pixel artist. If Square closed, Kazuko would have to switch jobs. Again. She didn't want to, so she did what she does best: created fantastic art and animation she hoped would draw in the audience *Final Fantasy* desperately needed.

Creating game art is never easy, but creating it on early consoles was especially challenging because of the technical limitations. Kazuko was limited by the color palette the Famicom could display, only twenty-five colors on-screen at the same time. If that seems like a lot, consider how many colors can exist within a single shadow—dozens of shades of blue, gray, and black—let alone the character or creature that cast it. That's the box in which Kazuko had to work.

She was tasked with creating character pixel art, fonts, menus, chibi characters, animations, and even monster designs. To create them for *Final Fantasy*, Kazuko had two major influences to draw from: the art of Yoshitaka Amano, and other games of the genre. Yoshitaka Amano was the concept artist for *Final Fantasy*, and he created pages and pages of ideas for monsters and other creatures that could be included in the game. Kazuko pored over this art, studying his style and larger-than-life designs, trying to figure out how to recreate his work in a limited engine. Yoshitaka didn't have to worry about the technical limitations of the game or Famicom, but Kazuko did. Some art she recreated in pixel form, and others she designed from scratch.

The second influence was other fantasy games, like the 1986 hit *Dragon Quest*. *Dragon Quest* was made by Enix, and if you're thinking, "Wait! Enix . . . Square . . . Square Enix?!" You're right. The two studios merged in 2003 to become Square Enix, one of the most well-known and profitable video game publishers in the world. But in 1984, Square and Enix were *fierce* competitors. Kazuko was studying *Dragon Quest*'s characters to see the kind of competition she was up against while creating animations for Square. A character in periwinkle blue armor takes his place on the screen.

His arms shift from side to side like someone doing capoeira or a very restrained dance move. His feet hop up and down, never resting. When he does move, it's less like walking and more like a moon walk: sliding side to side, up and down, his feet setting a rhythm totally different from the rest of his body. He is the star of *Dragon Quest*, a hero for the ages, the one fated to defeat the Dragonlord and save the princess.

Seeing him, Kazuko thought, "Huh. Why is he doing a crab walk?"

SIDE QUEST — SUSAN KARE

Graphic designer, artist, painter, and iconographer. Icono-what now? Susan Kare created what many designers call "proto-emojis," early icons that inspired the emojis we all use today in place of words. She also created the designs for the playing cards in *Solitaire*, the computer game thousands of office workers of the 1990s spent their time playing instead of, you know, working. No judgment here. Her design defined the look and feel of one of the most popular games ever created. Years later, she even released a real-life card deck that featured her designs for the cards that appear in *Solitaire*.

She also worked at Apple during its early days. When she started in 1982, she was tasked with making the Apple computer seem more "friendly" by creating appealing fonts and icons. In the words of the people who worked with her, Susan is the designer who "gave the Macintosh a smile."

The End of the End Times

Final Fantasy's opening cutscene and menu—Kazuko's creations—are iconic in the world of video games. A turreted gray castle stands proud among tiny cottages ringed by hedges. There are two massive bodies of water, connected by a river, that separate the castle from a peninsula of brilliant green earth. A pixelated character, who walks in a distinctly *not-crablike* way, crosses a bridge. The world shifts into black shadows and neon pink, green, and orange water. Four heroes stand on a hill beside a lake. A cape blows in the breeze and birds wheel overhead. The title appears: "FINAL FANTASY," in elegant blue and purple.

To create the scene, Kazuko needed to get by with, in her own words, "major economizing." Kazuko had the technical and artistic know-how to create the scene, from her time in anime, but couldn't use the same technology that worked in television. Early consoles had limited horsepower to display things like colors, let alone loading physics, animations, and music. Game animation wasn't even considered its own field yet. Kazuko came up with shortcuts and tricks to load in just enough information that wouldn't overwhelm the console, controlling where the camera was pointed so the player would, hopefully, not notice. "It turned out that working within such limited means was a good thing for me," she said in the 2013 *4gamer* interview. The challenge pushed her to create art and animation the gaming world had never seen before.

It was a good thing for the game, too. *Final Fantasy* was praised for its art, story, design, animation, monsters—basically, for the whole package. It sold more than 500,000 copies, and Square soon greenlit a sequel. Despite the first game's success, fewer than a dozen people were assigned to *Final Fantasy II*, and Kazuko was one of them. The whole team worked together in a room so small it could barely contain all their desks and chairs sitting back-to-back. "It was too small, so we were always fighting!" Kazuko told *4gamer*. "The programmers and the three of them in the middle were often quarreling."

It was only after *Final Fantasy II* sold as well as its predecessor that Square decided to add more people to the team. That gave Kazuko the time and resources she needed to create even more monsters, battle backgrounds, and maps than she'd been able to for the first two games. It also meant higher expectations, since the series' success was snowballing, drawing in more players than ever before. The monsters and creatures Yoshitaka Amano created were even bigger and more fantastic, and Kazuko wanted to capture them for *Final Fantasy III*. In many cases, that meant she needed to entirely redesign them to work on the console and fit the screen size. She succeeded, and *Final Fantasy III* continued to catapult the series' success.

It's hard to overstate how much of an impact not just the original *Final Fantasy* game but the entire series has had on the video game industry. There are fourteen main games and many more spinoffs, which have earned roughly $10.9 billion as of 2019. Along with the games, there is a wide range of additional *Final Fantasy* media and collectibles, from anime, manga, and novels to figurines, plushies, clothes, keychains, and so much more. Without *Final Fantasy*, we wouldn't have equally beloved series like *Kingdom Hearts*, *Mana*, and so many more.

The days of it feeling like the "end times" at Square were over.

Leading from the Background

In her thirty-plus years in the industry, Kazuko Shibuya has made more than thirty video games and contributed as a graphic designer, director, character artist, and supervisor. Yet she doesn't hold the same near-mythic place in the industry as the men she worked alongside when creating *Final Fantasy*, largely because she wasn't credited for her work until years later. Partly because of this, she's had fewer chances to speak publicly or in interviews. It wasn't until 2019, after she spoke at Japan Expo in Paris, France, that she was invited to be a member of Women in Games, a community interest group for, you guessed it, women who make, support, and play video games.

Even so, Kazuko has always been generous with advice. She gives it freely to artists, aspiring game developers, and really anyone interested in her work. She's written blogs and has risen to art director at Square Enix while mentoring upcoming artists. Her first piece of advice? Start with the fundamentals.

She also urges artists to get up from their desks and explore the world around them. To create fantasy or real worlds, artists need inspiration. Kazuko climbed Uluru, the sandstone monolith in Australia, and watched a sunset over a New Zealand mountain range. These are the moments and colors that live in her mind when she creates fantastical scenes and creatures, both in *Final Fantasy* and beyond. "There's no substitute for experiencing things with your own two eyes, taking in the whole atmosphere and context directly," she said. "A designer must hone all five of her senses. Vision, hearing, and smell and touch, too. They are all connected to creativity. The more experiences you have to draw from, the more depth you will be able to impart to your creations."

SIDE QUEST

KAREN LAUR

If you poke around in *Half-Life*'s Sector C, you'll find a row of lockers inscribed with names. One of them is Karen Laur, who was a texture artist on *Half-Life*. Texture artists make smooth 3D models look like real objects—adding wood grain to an in-game table, for example, or creating blades of grass along the ground. Karen joined Valve, the video game studio best known for *Half-Life* and *Left 4 Dead*, in 1997 and worked there for two years. Without her, *Half-Life* wouldn't have had the grounded look and feel that made it so spooky.

ROBIN HUNICKE

Game developer, researcher,
professor who speaks truth to power

I T'S HARD TO capture in words the disorganized, energetic, cheerful, manic chaos of the Game Developers Conference (GDC). It's the biggest educational gathering of developers in the world, and thousands of people descend on San Francisco every spring to learn, meet, and party. Game studios advertise upcoming titles and recruit talent; publishers try to persuade devs to use their products; and many gamedevs treat it as a massive family reunion.

One of the many draws to GDC are the panels, where you can learn everything from how to animate a giraffe to how one team made their game's shrink-gun work. Some panels are about learning new skills, while others are retrospectives on a specific game. Still others are about the state of the video game industry and the culture that surrounds it. The 2006 "Burn Baby, Burn: Developers Rant" fell firmly into that last category. Developers were handed a mic and told to rant about anything that bothered them. The hope was that the people in the audience, the present and future devs of the industry, would fix those things, or at least notice them. Up first: Frank Lantz, then a game designer and cofounder of Area/Code.

Frank stepped up to the mic, prompting a round of applause. As it faded, he opened with a surprise. "Before I begin, I am going to sublease one minute of my allotted five-minute rant." Enter, Robin Hunicke.

One minute isn't much, so Robin dove right in. Making games is hard, she said. "I came to this conference to see 'what's next?'" The crowd laughed, applauded, and whooped. Robin

described the talks she'd attended, the lessons she'd learned from people like Will Wright and Satoru Iwata, and how listening to them was simultaneously intimidating, inspiring, and exhausting. However, there was one thing about the conference that stood out to Robin, and not in the good way.

A quick reminder: GDC is a professional convention for game makers, not a commercial trying to *sell* games. It's meant to be educational, not entertaining. Yet the art hanging throughout the convention, meant to show off what companies and game schools thought was "next" for video games, didn't feel inspirational or professional at all.

"HOT CHICKS!" Robin shouted. "Give it up!"

Then Robin quickly listed the types of game art displayed in hallways: "Sexy babes who can't stop touching themselves. Coy babes who are kinda naked. Lesbian baaaaaabes. Studded babes!" In a whisper, "Latex babes."

"I just wanted to give you guys a huge shout-out," Robin said, her voice dripping with disdain, "because when I'm trying to recruit the next generation of developers who will expand our market and help us reach women gamers, how did I know that the best way to do it was just to prove to them that all of our characters are hot babes? It's been in front of me this whole time, and I COULDN'T EVEN SEE IT. Thank you."

Then she flipped the audience a set of double birds and walked off the stage.

Before the Birds

That wasn't Robin's first GDC, and it would be far from her last. By the time Robin was flipping off the audience to cap off her one-minute rant, she was already an award-winning designer, producer, and businesswoman.

Robin worked in artificial intelligence until 2005, when she met *Sims* director and video game legend Will Wright. From there, she joined Electronic Arts—one of the biggest companies in the biz both then and now—and became a designer on the expansion pack *The Sims 2: Open for Business*, was a lead designer on *MySims* for the Nintendo Wii, and worked as a producer on *Boom Blox* and its sequel. She eventually left Electronic Arts to join thatgamecompany, where she worked as a producer on the studio's third project, *Journey*. Released in 2012, the game won a slew of awards and became the company's most well-known game.

In a 2012 interview with the Smithsonian American Art Museum, Robin spoke about *Journey* alongside Kellee Santiago, cofounder and president of thatgamecompany, and Jenova Chen, cofounder and creative director. One of the groundbreaking elements of *Journey* is that it paired strangers together in an open space filled with beautiful music and ruins. The game allows players to interact with each other, but without chat or voice. To communicate, players "call" to each other with musical sounds, and when two players draw near each another, they glow.

The entire premise is an elegant, creative solution to a common problem in multiplayer games: how to keep players from bullying each other. For many other games, the answer to this is through tireless and constant community management. For *Journey*, the answer was to change how people communicate. "There was a moment between these two players where they were dancing on the air together," Robin said. "They had no idea who they were playing with. No one in the world had seen this experience before. And when I saw these two playtesters dancing like that together, I thought, that is something that is going to be really, really emotional for someone."

Robin eventually left thatgamecompany, cofounded a studio called Funomena, and worked on several titles, including the 2017 virtual reality game *Luna* and 2019's *Wattam*, for which she collaborated with *Katamari Damacy* creator Keita Takahashi. In 2008, Robin was named "Gamasutra's 20," which honors the "Top 20" people working in video games. She's received awards from Microsoft and *Edge* magazine, has taught courses in game design, served on awards juries, and founded a special interest group through the International Game Developers Association (IGDA). In short, she's one of the most well-regarded and socially active game developers out there.

But with great influence comes great responsibility (that's not quite how the Spider-Man saying goes, but roll with it), and Robin has consistently used her voice and influence to call out the continued lack of diversity in game development and the flimsy attempts to address it. At a GDC conference a few years after her iconic 2006 rant, she addressed the topic of diversity again, saying, "You are working actively to broaden participation in our industry, or you are in the way."

More Than Hot Babes

Robin often talks about the idea of hiring underrepresented creators as a "band-aid." Here's what that means: A team of white men is making a game, and they realize the game is appealing only to other white men and boys. So they hire someone who isn't a white man: a woman (usually a white one) or a creator of color (usually a man). Rarely, they hire a non-cis-male creator of color. Maybe a very talented one, maybe a very experienced one, but just *one*, and their job is to be the "band-aid," the one who will make a few quick fixes that make the game more appealing to more people. Done, diversity solved. But that doesn't actually *fix* the issue of making games with homogenous teams: it just puts all the responsibility on one person's shoulders, a person often used as a shield against criticism. It isn't right or fair, especially when the hired person feels disempowered to make any real changes.

Robin has spoken about this many times in her career, and in 2010, she gave one of her most comprehensive talks about it. Robin was invited to speak on a panel called Indie Gamemaker Rant!, a spiritual successor to "Burn Baby, Burn." She came prepared with numbers and research on why the band-aid approach doesn't work, and why studios fail to keep their diverse candidates around for very long.

Every year, the IGDA and GDC take surveys to get a good look at who is making games—measuring by gender, race, age, country of origin, and more—and whether they're happy. Robin reviewed five years' worth of surveys, and in every year, the percentage of women game designers was . . . drumroll please . . . 5 percent.

Yeah, you read that right. Five percent. It's true that "designer" is a specific title and doesn't include all of the other women working in the industry: artists, programmers, community managers, or writers, like yours truly. But still, 5 percent of designers? That's a bad look.

There are solutions, Robin said, but first people need to understand the problem. She recommended Virginia Valian's book *Why So Slow?*, which talks about the mind games people play with one another in professional settings: hidden expectations and power plays that hold back underrepresented people across many industries, including games. "And, really, these are culture problems," Robin said, "and, y'know, hey, that's not our problem, right? Except that games are culture."

Mic drop.

After reading *Why So Slow?*, Robin e-mailed Mary C. Murphy, PhD, then an assistant professor of psychology at the University of Illinois–Chicago and currently a professor and associate vice provost at Indiana University–Bloomington (that's where I went to college! You go, Mary!). Robin wanted to understand how people interact with one another in groups so she could better talk about these issues. That led her to the idea of "signaling threat," the focus of Dr. Murphy's research. In a Stanford University study, Dr. Murphy recruited students from math, science, and engineering programs and divided them into two groups: one that was half men and half women, and one where men outnumbered women three-to-one. Then both groups watched a video and were asked to discuss it. Dr. Murphy's team studied their skin responses, heart responses, senses of belonging, and willingness to participate in the discussion.

The study's findings? The women in the three-to-one group had faster heart rates, faster skin conductance, lower sense of belonging, and less desire to participate than the evenly divided group. They were more hyperaware of things around them, and as a result the women didn't remember much of the video they'd watched. "That's signal threat," Robin said. It's what happens when a small number of women (or just one) are put onto a team where they're badly outnumbered by men. It's one of the reasons women and BIPOC leave teams, especially when they were hired to be a "band-aid."

"We design feedback and reward systems for a living," Robin said. "We are young and motivated and trying to make a difference in this world. We can solve this problem. We need to get educated and try something."

She paused.

"Because I'm not a band-aid, and your games will be awesome if you do it."

KELLEE SANTIAGO

SIDE QUEST

The cofounder of thatgamecompany designs games like this: she starts with emotion and builds from there. It's a unique approach that's led to award-winning, genre-defining games like *Journey*. Born in Venezuela and raised in Virginia, computers were always a big part of Kellee Santiago's life. In college she studied experimental theater, and in graduate school she focused on interactive media. She was inspired by Tracy Fullerton, an experimental game designer and academic, and others who combine the artistry of theater with the technical savvy and interaction of computers.

KEIKO ERIKAWA

Creator of a genre, a company, and a mindset

A LITTLE GIRL SITS reading in her bedroom. It's dark outside, but she doesn't mind: she loves to study, and she has the light on. That is, until her mother catches her. Mom turns the light off, hoping her daughter will give up on the idea of an education. Spoilers, she won't.

This was one of many tiny wars Keiko Erikawa would fight in her life. Then when Keiko told her family she wanted to go to medical school, they urged her not to go to college and to get married instead. Later, she found herself the only woman in a male-dominated company and industry, so she invented an entirely new genre of games.

Yes, you read that right. Otome games, many of which are dating sims or feature romantic stories, exist because of Keiko. It seems fitting, then, that Keiko's career in video games also began with a love story.

The Dream Box

From the time she was small, Keiko was a romantic and a daydreamer. She loved to read, study, and paint, and she dreamed about marrying a French prince who would ride in on a white steed and shower her with riches. But when she was still a little girl, her life was abruptly uprooted: her father died, and she and her mother moved to her grandparents' rural home. She was bullied in her new school and neighborhood, but she didn't want to turn to adults for help, so she often took one of her grandparents' dogs with her on the two-mile walk to school. Keiko was learning to rely on herself, a lesson she would carry with her for many years to come.

Keiko's family discouraged her from going to college, instead urging her to get married as soon as possible. She ignored the advice and applied to the fashion design program at Tama Art University. While studying there, she met Yōichi Erikawa (later known as Kou Shibusawa), and before long, Yōichi was smitten. When Keiko's grandparents decided to rent out the top floors of their home, Yōichi applied to live there. He was boarding in their home when he confessed his love for Keiko. She later told the Japanese website *Entertainment Station* that "[Yōichi's parents] said that the daughter of boarding rooms had dangled a fishing line out the second floor and had, regrettably, reeled something in." There was a good deal of tension between their families, but nevertheless, Keiko and Yōichi married.

Not long after, it was her husband's birthday, and Keiko was desperate to cheer him up. The couple had recently taken over Keiko's in-laws' rural dyestuffs business. The work didn't suit her husband; he spent days poring over paperwork that didn't interest him at all. He carried around a "dream box" full of ideas and goals he'd written down, but he didn't trust himself to pursue them.

Keiko's dream box wasn't physical, as her husband's was, but she'd nonetheless needed to cling to her dreams and fight for them all of her life. Now she needed to help her husband do the same. The couple didn't have much money, but Keiko thought the occasion was worth splurging a little: she bought her husband a Sharp MZ, one of the first gaming computers released in Japan. He loved it, and it was exactly the push he needed.

After Keiko bought Yōichi a computer, he decided to study programming. That would lead to their next business venture, which had absolutely nothing to do with dyestuffs. It was something that interested both of them slightly more: a computer and software company. Eventually, a video game studio.

Seduction and Ambition

Keiko and her husband didn't set out to make games when they founded Koei in 1978. They focused on personal computers and software, but then Yōichi decided to try his hand at the same kind of project many software programmers were trying in the late 1970s: a video game. In 1982, Koei released its first video game, *Danchizuma no Yuuwaku*, 団地妻の誘惑, *Seduction of Condominium Wives*. It's one of the first Japanese RPGs, a role-playing game in which a door-to-door salesman tries to sell condoms to women and fights Yakuza and ghosts. Yeah, it's got a lot going on, and it was successful enough that people started to recognize the name "Koei."

A year after *Seduction*, Koei released *Nobunaga no Yabō*, 信長の野望, *Nobunaga's Ambition*, a strategy game set in Japan's Sengoku period. This was the post-feudal period between 1467 and 1615 when Japan was embroiled in near-constant civil war between clans and local lords. The game focused on resource management and tactical choices, and the strategy elements delighted players and won Koei acclaim. *Nobunaga* launched a sixteen-game series that's sold more than 10 million copies, across all titles worldwide, as of 2018.

By the early 1980s, Koei had established itself as a respected studio and creator of brilliant strategy games. Yet Keiko noticed something was missing: women. She was the only woman working on games at Koei, and that was evident not only behind-the-scenes, but in the types of games being greenlit, created, and marketed. Keiko wanted to make games that leaned away from the violence and competition already starting to dominate the games industry in the 1980s. She wanted to make a game that would've appealed to her as a little girl: something that appealed to her love of romance while being challenging. She wanted to make games for and about women—and she wanted to find women to make them.

Queen of Gems

Finding women to staff a new division at Koei wasn't easy. Because women weren't being actively recruited to programming schools and game studios—or, worse, discouraged from trying either—they weren't getting the experience that their male counterparts were able to list on a résumé. Keiko realized that and, rather than look solely at their past work experience, she decided to take a different approach. She interviewed women who had studied fields in the humanities: history, literature, anthropology, theater, theology, and more. There were more women with backgrounds in these areas, and Keiko knew she'd be able to teach women to use her studio's tools and technology after she'd recruited them. What she couldn't train was passion, creativity, interest, and ethics, all qualities they would've learned in the humanities. To Keiko, a potential hire's background made less of a difference than their interest and willingness to learn.

Over time, Keiko built a team of mostly women and formed Koei's new division: Ruby Party. Even the name was meant to be welcoming. Ruby, according to Keiko, is the "queen of jewels," and "party" was meant to sound friendly to people who had never made or played games before.

Though Keiko was confident in her hires and in her new division, they were under a ton of pressure from the get-go. She was trying to prove a hypothesis few other studios and publishers were even interested in exploring: that games made by and marketed to women could sell well. Every norm and best practice designed with men in mind had to be tossed out. Ruby Party needed to create something new and accessible. They needed to invent a whole new genre of video games.

Queen of the Cosmos

We know, thanks to survey creators and survey takers, that women play all sorts of games. They play Match-3 games, MMOs, RPGs, shooters, puzzles, roguelikes, and sandboxes.

> ⇒ **MATCH-3:** Also called tile-matching games. *Candy Crush*, *Bejeweled*, and *Tetris* fall under this category.

> ⇒ **MMO:** Massively multiplayer online. Includes games like *RuneScape*, *Elder Scrolls Online*, *World of Warcraft*, and *Guild Wars*.

> ⇒ **RPG:** Role-playing game. See a longer definition in the glossary on page XI!

> ⇒ **SHOOTER:** FPS, or first-person shooter, falls under this category. *Asteroids*, *Centipede*, *Call of Duty*, *Doom Eternal*, and *Destiny* are all shooters.

> ⇒ **PUZZLE:** The broadest of these categories, puzzle refers to any game that's about solving logic problems. *Tetris*, *Sudoku*, *Candy Crush Saga*, and *Portal* are puzzle games.

➡ **ROGUELIKE:** See this definition in the glossary on page XI!

➡ **SANDBOX:** A game in which the player is free to explore a map, or the "sandbox," to play in. Deemphasizes specific goals and lets players roam free, affecting the environment. Think *Minecraft, No Man's Sky,* and *Grand Theft Auto.*

They are more likely to play games in which women feature prominently, or games in which players can customize their main characters and choose their gender. Women are most likely to play games that are marketed toward them: those that feature women on the box, in the marketing campaigns, and in the trailers. Even before we knew all this, Keiko was sure that women gamers were out there; Ruby Party just needed to find them.

When Ruby Party started work on *Angelique* in 1990, they had none of the data above to draw from. As the director of the project, Keiko decided to start with what she already knew: *Nobunaga's Ambition's* strategy-game mechanics. Simultaneously, the Ruby Party team looked at manga and anime for women. Keiko was sure that a well-designed strategy game with the right aesthetic and story—inspired by shōjo manga and anime in both its look and storytelling—could make a great game for and about women.

In *Angelique,* two high-school girls compete to become Queen of the Cosmos. One of them—you, the player—is Angelique, and you have to prove your worthiness by ruling a nation and managing its resources capably. You can ask any of the nine "guardians," all men, for help to win the competition. The story and art of the game lean heavily on shōjo manga influences, like the 1970s series *Candy Candy,* from which Ruby Party drew the design of their main character. The nine guardians are all influenced by Greek mythology, which is another common storytelling device in shōjo manga.

Once an early version of the game was built, the Ruby Party team put it in front of play-testers. These are people invited to play early "builds" of a game and asked to give their feedback. Are the mechanics fun or tedious? Are the goals obvious or murky? Is the dialogue charming or grating? These are the kinds of questions playtesters are asked, and their feedback shapes the future of a game. I speak from experience here (thank you, playtesters!). For *Angelique,* Keiko brought in a playtester she knew would be brutally honest with the team: her daughter, Mei.

Mei's assessment?

Boring. Ordering the guardians around wasn't fun, the story didn't hold her interest for long, and there was no romance element.

Keiko and the Ruby Party team took the feedback seriously and brainstormed how to make the game more fun and engaging. They tweaked the mechanics and story surrounding the competition between Angelique and her in-game rival. And, critically, they added romance: Angelique could fall in love with one of the nine guardians instructed to help her.

After months of rebooting the game with new features and story, Keiko was ready to share the game with Mei again. The team braced for Mei's reaction.

Mei adored it.

With this seal of approval, Keiko knew that *Angelique* was ready for the market. It was an incredibly stressful and uncertain time, as Keiko and the team waited to see if their passion, hard work, and risk would pay off. Would *Angelique* be the game that would entice and resonate with women gamers and make them invest in a Nintendo game console and pick up the game? Of course, we know the answer to these questions, and soon so did Ruby Party. And the answer was an incredibly firm *yes*.

The Ruby Party team had created an entirely new genre, one that focused on women as its target audience, leaned on story, and centered on romantic choices. Otome has had a massive impact on video games not just in Japan, but worldwide. Series like *Final Fantasy* and *Persona* added otome elements, like romance and high-school protagonists, to later titles, and *Dream Daddy* probably wouldn't exist without otome.

In 1994, ten years after Keiko decided to create Ruby Party, *Angelique* shipped for the Super Famicom, also called the Super NES. It wasn't an instant hit, but Keiko wasn't willing to give up on it. She knew girls simply didn't know about the game, so she planned manga tie-ins and drama CDs to flesh out the story of the world and characters. It worked, and over time, *Angelique* sold so well that it spawned four sequels, three spinoffs, and multiple manga and anime tie-ins to the *Angelique* universe.

Most importantly, the wide success of *Angelique* proved Keiko's hypothesis that women could *make* games, and women would *buy* games designed for them. "There were some who said, 'The market is small. If you make games for women, they won't sell,'" Keiko Erikawa told *Famitsu* in 2015. "But I thought, 'The market is there.' I'm glad I stuck to my conviction."

CHRISTINE LOVE

In 2016, there was exactly one game everyone on GDC's indie floor was buzzing about: *Ladykiller in a Bind*. This risqué visual novel-slash-dating simulator starred a queer woman, was written by a queer woman, and explored consent, social status, and BDSM. The creative mind behind this groundbreaking game belongs to Christine Love. Christine's games focus on gender, sexuality, and the role of technology in social situations, as well as how to explore more adult topics through games. Her games follow many of the romance/dating sim norms established in the otome genre, but she uses them to explore topics like kink and consent. Christine is one of the most popular indie devs in the business, and any time she releases a game, you can bet *everyone* will be talking about it.

"Live Large and Live Long"

Both of Keiko's daughters would eventually work for Koei. Mei Erikawa, the one who had given *Angelique* such crucial feedback, eventually became director of the Ruby Party brand. That means she helps guide creative decisions for Ruby Party—definitely a good fit for such a valuable playtester.

Keiko was Koei's executive director until 2002, but she remained the honorary chair of the board of directors for several years after. In 2009, a merger began between Koei and Tecmo. After a series of purchases, acquisitions, mergers, and sales that took several years, the two became Koei Tecmo.

In the years after *Angelique*, Keiko prioritized making her now-massive company a positive and inclusive place to work. She boasts that turnover—which is the rate at which people are hired, quit, and replaced—is lower at Koei Tecmo than the national average. The number of mothers and fathers who take family leave is also considerably better. "As a female manager who has been engaged in business," Keiko wrote on Koei's website, "I also expect women to play an active role. Half of the world is women. If men and women with different thoughts and sensibilities complement each other . . . the possibilities are endless."

Keiko encouraged all creators to challenge themselves and feel the joy that comes with self-actualization—and she would know. At the end of the game, Angelique becomes queen of the cosmos, and Keiko is the crowned queen of the otome genre. And it all started because when someone decided to turn off the light, Keiko turned it back on: for herself and for anyone who's ever been discouraged from pursuing their dreams.

BRENDA LAUREL

Game designer, researcher,
and entrepreneur in utopia

ABOUT A MONTH before I started making AAA games, a man asked me to work on a project that wasn't a video game (and wasn't this book, either). While trying to persuade me to leave video games for good, he said, "Don't you wanna write for someone besides sixteen-year-old boys?"

You probably already know this, wise reader, but just to say it again: video games aren't just for sixteen-year-old boys, and if this book has taught you anything, it is that they *never have been*. But in the early 1990s, a lot of game designers, much like the guy above, still thought of teenage boys as their *only* audience. The way most games were marketed, their names, their main characters—they were all designed in answer to the question "What would boys like to play?" Most games, that is, except for the ones designed by Brenda Laurel.

Games for Girls, By Girls

Like many game designers of the 1980s and '90s, Brenda did a little bit of everything, from design to programming to production management. She worked as a producer at Atari from 1980 until 1983, and she earned a doctorate degree from Ohio State University and wrote a thesis that turned into her 1991 book, *Computers as Theatre*.

Throughout her journey, Brenda kept coming back to a two-part question: "Why were so few studios designing games for girls?" and "Was making the box pink"—as Barbie was aggressively marketed—"really the only way to appeal to young women?" Brenda lost more than one job for suggesting that games could be more than just shooting and fighting and could reach a wider audience than little boys. "It can't just be a giant sexist conspiracy," Brenda said in a retrospective 1998 TED Talk. "These people aren't that smart. There's $6 billion on the table. They would go for it if they could figure out how." For the next decade, the heart of Brenda's work was dedicated to answering these questions: What would it take to build a studio dedicated to making games for girls? And what should games for girls *look* like?

Purple/Pink on the Move

Before we dive into Brenda's research, the "purple games movement," and the question of what young girls want to play, let's take a quick aside to talk about gender. In the United States, the market and society where Brenda was operating, our understanding of gender has changed since the 1990s. Gender isn't as simple as the binary categories of "male" and "female," but encompasses a much broader palette that includes "nonbinary," "gender fluid," "Two Spirit," and more. Furthermore, many of the things we see as gendered, like clothes and taste in movies, are *norms*, not *truths*. There is no reason boys can't like sparkly nail polish, just as there's no reason girls won't play with toy monster trucks. It's a complicated issue that ties into modeling behavior, gender performance, and other terms studied extensively by sociologists and psychologists. I bring all this up because Brenda's research focused entirely on gender and was set against the backdrop of the 1990s, the era of Toni Morrison (first Black woman to win the Nobel Prize in Literature, plus a Pulitzer Prize and Presidential Medal of Freedom), Sally Ride (the first woman to go to space), and Madeleine Albright (first woman to serve as US Secretary of State). The question of the era was, "how do we invite women and girls into male-dominated spaces?" Brenda's own views on gender and gameplay have changed since the 1990s, but she stands by the research that created Purple Moon. Okay, back to Brenda's story.

The first step in understanding what little girls would play was to look at the games already made for them. Brenda started with the *Barbie* game created for the Commodore 64, an early computer. It was designed and marketed for little girls, which in this case meant taking common mechanics like shooting and slowing them *waaaaay dowwwwn*. Why? Well, gamedevs "knew" girls were bad at shooters (*ugh, no*), so they figured slowing the bullets down would allow girls to play. Rather than asking girls what interested them, they just made a slower, less-fun version of a mechanic they'd been aggressively marketing to boys for years. That plus drenching the box in pink and rebranding the bullets as "marshmallows" equals *girl game*.

Brenda wanted to dig deeper. Was it enough to just tweak or simplify already existing mechanics, or were there different types of gameplay that would have a broader appeal among young girls? In a 1997 *Wired* article, Brenda said, "The game business arose from computer programs that were written by and for young men in the late 1960s and early 1970s. They worked so well that they formed a very lucrative industry fairly quickly. But what worked for that demographic absolutely did not work for most girls and women."

Brenda didn't want to make "girl games" that were slowed-down versions of popular "boy games." She didn't want to stick them in pink boxes and say "good enough." Luckily, she wasn't the only one asking why no one was interested in expanding games' audience to young girls. In 1992, Brenda met computer scientist David Liddle at a conference. Liddle and his business partner, Microsoft cofounder Paul Allen, were creating the Interval Research Corporation to study how people interacted with technology. When Brenda asked Liddle why no one was trying to make games for little girls, he didn't know the answer, either, so he hired Brenda to figure it out.

There was one hard rule established by Paul Allen and David Liddle before Brenda got to work: whatever the research said little girls wanted, those were the games Brenda would make—even if it was games with slowed-down marshmallow guns in pink boxes.

Partnering with some of the best researchers in the world, Brenda learned how to answer the questions that had been bouncing around in her head for years. "They taught me how to look and see," Brenda said in a 1998 TED Talk, "and they did not do the incredibly stupid thing of saying to a child, 'Of all these things we already make, which do you like best?'—which gives you zero answers that are usable." Brenda spent two and a half years in initial research and another year and a half in "advance development" to discover what young girls wanted in their games. She and her team studied literature, cognitive psychology, spatial cognition, gender studies, play theory, sociology, and primatology—yes, the study of monkeys. Specifically, they studied Frans de Waal's work about how monkeys behave in social groups, which greatly influenced Brenda's game design. "Thank you Frans de Waal, wherever you are," Brenda said in the TED Talk, "I love you, and I'd give anything to meet you."

After two years of research, Brenda's team began "the heart of the work." They interviewed more than 1,000 children of multiple genders between the ages of seven and twelve, then they conducted surveys of 10,000 more children and studied the results. What they found was that, broadly speaking, little girls wanted *stories*. They were drawn to relatable characters, complex social interactions, and introspective gameplay that asked them what they thought and felt instead of just telling them what to do. With that knowledge and Interval's support, Brenda founded a studio that would create games focused on those things: Purple Moon.

Of course, Brenda and her team didn't exist in a creative vacuum. As the team completed their research and shifted into their first production phase, several companies had also joined the "games for girls" movement. In 1996, a year before Purple Moon would launch its first two games, Mattel shipped *Barbie Fashion Designer* in a huge, bright pink box. In its first two months on the shelves, the game sold more than half a million copies and eventually outsold games like *Doom* and *Quake*. In the wake of that success, *Barbie Fashion Designer* was called the "first commercially successful video game made for girls."

As the Games for Girls movement gained momentum, different studios and publishers took different approaches to reach young girls and women. Some, like Mattel, stayed pink and sparkly. Others shifted focus to stories, characters, and mysteries, like Her Interactive (you can read more about their *Nancy Drew* games in Megan Gaiser's chapter on page 112), Girl Games, and Broderbund. Broderbund's *Carmen Sandiego* series appealed to both girls and boys, making the titular character an instant classic. Her Interactive's *McKenzie and Co.*, a game about trying to land a date for prom, sold a respectable 40,000 copies in less than three years, and the *Nancy Drew* series would go on to sell millions of copies. This split the movement into two halves: the "pink games movement" and the "purple games movement." Brenda was one of the leaders of the latter, which is how Purple Moon got its name.

"The problem wasn't that girls didn't want games," said game designer Sheri Graner Ray around the same time (you can read more about her on page 126), "it was that they couldn't *find* them. Girls don't shop at software stores, they don't read computer game magazines. Where do you put your ads?" Responding to a question about whether the Games for Girls movement would force girl-focused studios to compete with one another, Sheri added, "When I walk into a software store, and I see an entire aisle full of software for girls, then I'll worry about competition. At this point, we're all trying to help each other stay alive."

New (Purple) Moon

After thousands of interviews, surveys, and hours of research, Purple Moon shipped its first two games in 1997: *Rockett's New School* and *Secret Paths in the Forest*. Neither shipped in a pink box, and they incorporated dialogue options, which helped players focus more on the characters, social situations, and introspection. While it was a novelty when Purple Moon began designing the mechanic, it has since become an iconic, well-known design pillar for some of the most popular games ever created, including *Mass Effect*, *Dragon Age*, *Minecraft*, *Skyrim*, *StarCraft*, and *World of Warcraft*, to name just a few. It's easy to wonder how different those games would have been if the Purple Games Movement had never happened.

The opening of *Rockett's New School* goes like this: a red-haired girl's internal monologue begins: "Okay, did anyone ever say starting eighth grade at a new school would be like, smooth skateboarding on solid ground? No! But let's just hope I at least don't make some mega blunder on my very first day here." The school speaker blares, and the announcer tells everyone to "make new friends but keep the old." Rockett rolls her eyes. The game shifts into its first choice about how Rockett feels: Is she confident and excited, nervous but determined, or totally overwhelmed?

The second game, *Secret Paths in the Forest*, begins in a treehouse with a prominent sign: Girls Only. Seashells, flowers, books, and pillows are strewn across the wood floors; the background is watercolor-like swirls that suggest forests and mountains. A book adorned with a vivid purple heart invites the player to click on it, "The Book of the Secret Paths." "Dear Friend," the book reads, "I have no idea if anyone will ever find this secret journal, but something tells me I must leave it here, regardless . . ."

One game focused on the external lives of girls: parties, cliques, dances, and campfire secrets. The other explored their dreams, fantasies, and fears. Brenda's research had shown this was what broadly appealed to little girls, but now the success of her games would prove or cut against years of work. Would little girls actually pick up the games?

They sure did. In December 1997, *Rockett's New School* sold 39,174 copies, earning $1.1 million. *Entertainment Weekly* called the game "thoughtfully addictive." Though *Secret Paths in the Forest* sold fewer copies, it still did well, selling 23,539 copies in the same month. Over the next three years, Purple Moon shipped five more *Rockett* titles and three more *Secret Paths* games, plus a new game titled *Starfire Soccer Challenge*.

Alongside its games, Purple Moon launched another product that was ahead of its time: Purple-moon.com. Girls could log onto forums, bulletin boards, and chat rooms (with an adult's permission) to talk about their choices and characters. Before DeviantArt, Tumblr, and Reddit, there was purple-moon. Purple Moon had figured out how to foster an online community of gamer girls before anyone else had even tried.

Yet as Purple Moon grew in popularity and influence, adult gamers and reviewers began to criticize the games and the purpose of the studio. Some asked whether the games were enforcing gender stereotypes by focusing on things like cliques and relationships. As I said earlier, Brenda's views on the role of gender in play and video games has changed since the 1990s, but she's always responded to criticism of Purple Moon by saying: Purple Moon made games girls wanted, not the ones people thought they should have. Brenda was more interested in creating games that mirrored girls' daily lives and struggles, like peer pressure and how to navigate friendships, than trying to teach girls what they *should* care about. Still, she understands the criticism, though she thinks some of it is unfair. "By trying to do anything socially positive at all," she wrote in her book *Utopian Entrepreneur*, "the utopian entrepreneur opens herself up to the endless critique that she is in fact not doing enough."

SOHA EL-SABAAWI

We often hear about the different ways that studios fail either their employees or players—or hire women as band-aids, as Robin Hunicke has called out—but we rarely hear about the wins. Soha El-Sabaawi, Riot Games' first head of diversity, wants more victories. After company leaders at Riot were accused of harassment and creating a toxic work culture for women and other marginalized groups, Soha joined to try to fix it. "We wanted to be a better company," Soha told *Uproxx* in 2020. "It doesn't just end. This is an everyday movement. So that's been the biggest learning [curve] for all of us—you don't just fix it, and it's 'cool we solved the D&I issues.' Diversity changes. It's always evolving."

In Rockett's Wake

It was 1999, two years after *Rockett's New School* and *Secret Paths in the Forest* vaulted Purple Moon to become one of the leaders of the Purple Games Movement. In Brenda's living room were employees of Purple Moon gathered to hold a wake—a funeral—for Rockett Movado, the star of the *Rockett* series. A plastic Rockett doll was laid out in full ceremony, complete with purple irises, black candles, and Irish whiskey.

Soon, Purple Moon would be gone. Everyone at Purple Moon had already lost their jobs. What remained of the company would be bought by Mattel, the creators of Barbie. None of the Purple Moon founders or employees would make money off the sale. If you go to purple-moon.com today, you'll be redirected to Barbie's page on the Mattel website. Purple Moon was, according to Brenda, killed by one thing: the desire to protect Barbie.

Brenda delivered Rockett's final eulogy, saying, "We're always trying to heal something. Lousy childhoods, raw deals, crappy self-esteem. We were trying to heal something when we made her." Brenda raised her glass, and the crowd followed suit. "To the little redheaded girl."

Employees sobbed. Brenda's daughters carried the redheaded doll upstairs. Then from the staircase landing she descended: Rockett, dangling from a string, now clad in a hot-pink gown and feathered wings, an angel. The message was clear: Rockett and Purple Moon might be ending, but neither would ever really be *gone*.

Brenda's Utopia

The world of video games has changed since Brenda launched a massive research project trying to understand what girls wanted from video games. The Games for Girls movement of the 1990s is one of the reasons why.

"In a way, the need for the kind of cultural intervention we made with Purple Moon no longer exists, in that girls and women are full participants in the world of computer-based interactivity," Brenda said in an interview with TED in 2009. "But we still have a problem with female designers getting their work out there. And there are many genres and areas of interest for girls and women that remain untouched." She named some of her heroes in game design, like Tracy Fullerton, danah boyd*, Justine Cassell, and Henry Jenkins, who all "keep the flame burning for women in gaming."

"I think that the industry as a whole learned from the girl game movement that their audience could be much broader," Brenda said in an interview about Purple Moon's rise and fall. "I think that interventions like Purple Moon enhanced girls' comfort with computers, which we set out to do, and brought girls roaring into the online game space, eventually becoming major players in game worlds like *World of Warcraft* and, of course, *The Sims*."

After Purple Moon closed, Brenda became a chair at the nonprofit ArtCenter College of Design in California. She also taught at the California College of the Arts and the University of California, Santa Cruz, wrote books about business and design, and consulted for some of the biggest companies in the world, including Sony Pictures, Apple, and Citibank.

At her core, Brenda is a leader in business, in ethics, and in creativity. This comes across in every interview, article, and book written about or by her. The clearest vision of this is in her 2001 book *Utopian Entrepreneur*, in which she writes about her goals, dreams, moments of naiveté, and passion for creating ethical business: "I'm not unaware," Brenda wrote, "that combining 'utopia' with 'entrepreneur' creates something of an oxymoron." Her work was about change; not just making money, but improving culture.

That Purple Moon didn't survive doesn't change the fact that Brenda succeeded at her goal, and without her and "purple games," innovation in story and social navigation in games would be years behind where it is now. "Regardless of the fate of your businesses,"

* danah boyd spells her name with no capital letters.

Brenda wrote, "emerging with your health and heart intact will allow you to pursue another dream on another day. And remember: this is not your last idea."

This is not your last idea.

Purple Moon wasn't Brenda's first or last idea. Purple Moon created games that were popular, well-researched, innovative, and, at times, even controversial. It paved the way for a different kind of video game, one that focused on emotions and everyday problems. And it created a space for a different kind of gamer: one who wasn't a sixteen-year-old boy, but a girl between eight and fourteen years old. One who could love video games, and someday even make them. Just like Brenda herself.

AURICA HARVEY

The creator of art-games, not game-art

"Modern art tends to be ironical, cynical, self-referential,
afraid of beauty, afraid of meaning
—other than the trendy discourse of the day—"

"Go to them rather than expecting them to come to the museum.
Contemporary art is a style, a genre, a format.
Think!"

"Do not fear beauty.
Do not fear pleasure.
Make art-games, not game-art."

T HESE ARE EXCERPTS from the "Realtime Art Manifesto," written by Auriea Harvey and her husband, Michaël Samyn, in 2006, when they were the cofounders and directors of indie game studio Tale of Tales. The manifesto rejects the commercialism of major games and studios, praises the future of real-time 3D art ("the most remarkable new creative technology since oil on canvas," in their words), and questions the very term "game."

When digital art was still rare, Auriea Harvey became one of the first well-known artists on the 1990s internet. Now that digital art is ubiquitous, she's a sculptor living in Rome, a city famous for sculptures that date back thousands of years. She's had many different titles over the course of her career: digital artist, web developer, game designer, professor, sculptor. What unites them all is this: an understanding of her place not just in modern art and interactivity, but in the history of how people make and engage with art itself.

Classically Trained

From the time Auriea was a teenager, her jobs and interests pointed toward a career in art and interactivity. She was born in Indianapolis, Indiana, in 1971. At sixteen years old, she got a job in a framing store, where she looked at art all day. At eighteen, she worked at the Children's Museum of Indianapolis and helped design exhibits for kids.

One of the best places to learn game design is a theme park. Think about it: A theme park is a giant interactive space filled with things to do, with no one dictating in which order they should be done. If you want to ride Space Mountain twenty-six times, you can; that's why it's a useful tool for game designers to understand how to design a space that can be both enjoyable and completely up to its user. Museums are much the same way, with the added ingredient of education. Even before Auriea attended college, she was learning the tools and mindset to be a creator of interactive art—like a game designer.

After she graduated from high school, Auriea studied at one of the most prestigious art schools in the world, the Parsons School of Design in New York City. She was studying sculpture, but she was learning far more: she got a job working in the school's first-ever computer lab. It sparked an interest in technology that would eventually grow into a career as a game designer. She even taught herself to code and began creating websites. Before long, she had clients clamoring for her digital art and website design, including PBS and Virgin Records America. She later described it as abandoning the real world for hyperspace. But hyperspace—and romance—were about to change her real-world life forever.

PORPENTINE CHARITY HEARTSCAPE

Branching choices and dialogue options are among the most recognizable work game writers do, and in 2012, Porpentine Charity Heartscape changed how we think about them. She created a hypertext game called *Howling Dogs*, which called back to the early days of text-only game writing, like *Colossal Cave Adventure* (the game Roberta Williams played before she decided to make *Mystery House*). *Howling Dogs* was so gripping, poetic, and thoughtful, it was nominated alongside much larger, higher budget games for a variety of awards, including "best story" and "best writing."

A Meeting of the Minds (and Hearts)

Auriea and Michaël Samyn met in hell. That is, on a domain called hell.com, in an artists' collective, in 1999. To get an idea of what the internet looked like around that time, type in www.spacejam.com/1996. That's the original website for the 1996 movie starring Michael Jordan. Starry backgrounds, bulky icons, LiveJournals, message forums: these were the early, lawless days of the internet, and it's where Auriea and Michaël fell in love.

Both were digital artists, so it's no surprise their romance was digital, as well. They sent each other art and romantic, poetic messages. They created *Wirefire*, an "online performance engine" that combined chat, sounds, animations, images, and live streams, to better communicate with each other and audiences. They exchanged texts and images Michaël would later call their first collaborative project, *Skinonskinonskin*.

Their next project was a merger: Auriea had created her own website, *Entropy8*, in 1995, and Michaël, a programmer as well as an artist, had created *Zuper*. They squished them together to create *Entropy8Zuper!* the same year they met. "We decided to work together and to pretend we were not falling in love," Michaël told *Creative Capital* in an interview sixteen years later.

Though nothing stood between Auriea and Michaël online, a number of barriers separated them in real life. The first was distance: she lived in the United States, and he lived in Belgium. The second: they were both in relationships with other people, and Michaël had two small children. Still, a few months after they met online, they both—by chance—were traveling to San Francisco. After meeting in person, they realized there was no turning back: they were in love. They tried to break up with each other, failed, and a few months later, Auriea moved to Belgium. Michaël would later describe the speed of their courtship as somewhat rash, but successful: they're still together more than twenty years later—and among the most influential gamedevs and digital artists *ever*.

Interactive Displays

The first project Auriea and Michaël created together was called *The Godlove Museum*. It was a series of artwork hosted on the internet, a blend of personal, political, and social commentary interwoven with stories from the Bible. Auriea and Michaël created different "books" of the museum—Genesis, Exodus, Leviticus, Numbers, and Deuteronomy— over eight years, starting in 1999 and ending in 2006.

But Auriea and Michaël were becoming, for lack of a better word, bored with what the internet was turning into during the early 2000s. It had stopped feeling like a collective and started to feel more like a shopping mall. "Just CSS and databases," Auriea said in an interview with *Rock Paper Shotgun*. As they fell out of love with the internet, they were falling in love with something else: video games. On the night of their wedding, Auriea and Michaël took home a bottle of champagne and played *Tekken 3* together to celebrate, and they were stunned. They stopped renting movies together and started renting games instead. They played *Ico*, *Black & White*, *Silent Hill*, *Soul Calibur*, *Neverwinter Nights*, *Guild Wars*, *Ceremony of Innocence*, *Animal Crossing*, and more. They had a lot of opinions about the games they were playing, and eventually they thought, what if we made one?

What fascinated them about games were the immersive environments: the ability to lose themselves in a world and story. They liked interacting with creatures and becoming a different person. What they didn't like were rewards, challenges, skills, and goals. They didn't like competition. So when Auriea and Michaël started working on their first game, they abandoned all of those concepts in favor of an explorable, gentle space. Thus, *The Endless Forest* was born.

The Endless Forest is an appropriate name in more ways than one. It takes place in, as you might have guessed, a forest. The game is an MMORPG and was launched by Auriea and Michaël's newly founded studio, Tale of Tales, in 2005. In *The Endless Forest*, you play as a deer. You have no objectives, and there is no violence. There's no chat, voice or otherwise. You can communicate the way a deer would: roar, sniff, eat mushrooms, carry flowers, walk, nap. You can find and gather with other players, also deer, at landmarks like the Pond. Auriea and Michaël created weather systems and invited players to herd around—er, no pun intended—certain areas at certain times. The game is still playable today and was updated as recently as 2021—truly, an endless space.

The medium of video games was perfect for Auriea and Michaël. They'd lost faith in the internet of the early 2000s, but they didn't want to participate in what they called "the fine art system." They didn't want to have to go through museums, curators, galleries, or corporations to show their art. With *The Endless Forest*, they'd created interactive art with their audience directly. In an e-mail interview with *GameScenes*, they said, "We're enchanted by the intimacy of videogames."

CELIA PEARCE

In 2005, an idea dawned on game designer and academic Celia Pearce. She wanted to create a festival specifically for indie games. It would be a place where independent creators could show off their work, give awards for excellence, and network with other independent developers. The result was IndieCade, which some call "the video game industry's Sundance [Festival]." Celia is IndieCade's cofounder along with Stephanie Barish and Sam Roberts. She also designs everything from museum installations to a card game for Purple Moon, based on the *Rockett* series. Celia's work focuses on cosplay, role-playing, and the representation and performance of gender in video games.

Inspiring the Masses

One of the most fondly remembered—and subsequently copied—levels from a AAA game is the Tibetan village in *Uncharted 2: Among Thieves*. In the level, the main character wanders a village nestled in snow-covered mountains. It's one of the few times in the game that you're not shooting, jumping, running, or falling. Instead, you're trying to figure out where you are, and the village continues its daily life and business around you. It's one of the most immersive levels ever created in a blockbuster game, all the more effective because "slow" levels were and are pretty rare in action-adventure games.

That level exists because of an entirely different game: *The Graveyard*, created by Auriea and Michaël a year before *Uncharted 2* shipped. Naughty Dog designer Richard Lemarchand told *Gamasutra* that when he played *The Graveyard*, it affected him "much more than he expected." In *The Graveyard*, you control an elderly woman walking through a graveyard. There are no levels, no goals, no stats. There's no one you have to talk to. It's just a space to walk through and reflect. Richard wanted to create a similar emotion in *Uncharted*, and thus, the Tibetan village was born.

All of Auriea and Michaël's games honed in on a similar structure: to create a space for the player to *think*. Sometimes about death, as in *The Graveyard*. Sometimes about nature and community, as in *The Endless Forest*. In *The Path*, inspired by the Little Red Riding Hood fairy tale, the player is given only one objective: stay on the path. Whether they do or not determines the tone of the game: comforting or terrifying, welcoming or ominous.

Then in 2010, Auriea and Michaël gave a talk at Georgia Tech's Art History of Games Symposium called "Over games." They said that most video games were made to appeal to children, and not enough interactive, digital art was being created for adults. No wonder, then, that in 2013 Tale of Tales released a game very much for adults: *Luxuria Superbia*. The idea for the game began when Auriea and Michaël were in a roundtable discussion with Brenda Romero (also in this book! page 107) at GDC. Brenda asked, "What's the game mechanic for sex?" Auriea and Michaël became fascinated with the question, and a few years later, they released *Luxuria Superbia*, a game about sex that has nothing graphic in it. It's a collection of flowers, shapes, colors, circles, and eyes. The game is played with a touch-screen and responds to the ways the player touches the environments: touch it in the right way, and the score and environments respond.

After a little more than five years, and despite their struggles with the industry, Auriea and Michaël had drawn the eyes of developers and critics alike. Other game designers wanted to recapture the emotions and tone their games embodied; critics said their work expanded the idea of what games could be from toys to artwork.

Back to (Classical) Roots

Looking back, Frank Lantz (the former director of the NYU Game Center, in case you forgot) compares Auriea's early work with what would eventually be explored and beloved in narrative and walking simulation games like *Gone Home*, *Firewatch*, and *Beginner's Guide*. All of these games ignore the traditional measures of success players have come to expect when playing a video game, such as points, competition, explicit goals, and conflict, in favor of contemplation, exploration, and subtle storytelling. "A game can be anything," Auriea said at IndieCade, a festival that celebrates independent developers. There are no limits, she explained, to what constitutes a game, no constraints that define what shape the art has to take. Except one: "The artwork needs the audience to exist."

It wouldn't be accurate to say Auriea Harvey has left games entirely. *The Endless Forest* is still playable, and Michaël added updates to it as recently as 2021. Still, many articles about Auriea and her work refer to her as a "game designer turned sculptor," indicating she's no longer the former. Tale of Tales published its last game, *Sunset*, on May 21, 2015. Auriea called the end of her game design career "a happy divorce." Her goal had never been to make games for the purpose of selling them, and after making "unconventional" games for years, she was ready to try something new. "We are looking forward to working in media where we feel encouraged to explore, to experiment, to do things that have never done before," she told *Creative Capital*.

That's not to say Auriea never questioned her decision. A year after she shipped her last game, she gave a talk at the NYU Game Center and asked, "Have I chosen wrong, is my question? What have I been doing with my life?"

A lot, as it turns out. Auriea returned to her roots as a sculptor and lives in Rome, Italy. She sells 3D sculptures, talks about and creates art in augmented and virtual reality spaces, and loves to talk about her 3D printer. Before that, she became the first Professor of Games at Kunsthochschule Kassel, an almost three-hundred-year-old art institute in Germany. Through it all, what remains are the tenets she and her husband first laid out in their manifesto: to be creators of games-as-art, not art-for-games.

"Tell the story through interaction."

"Think poetry, not prose."

"Ignore the critics and the fanboys.
Make work for your audience instead."

"Step one: drop the requirement of making a game.
The game structure of rules and competition stands in the way of expressiveness.
Interactivity wants to be free."

AMY HENNIG

The filmmaker who made them interactive

D O GAMES REALLY need writers? You might be thinking, "Yes, obviously" (and bless you if you are), but this is a question that people within the industry still passionately debate, as if on cue, every few years. Ian Bogost wrote an, er, *divisive* 2017 article in *The Atlantic* titled "Video Games Are Better Without Stories." Auriea Harvey made it clear, at least in 2006, that she was more interested in interactive, open spaces than authored game experiences. And more recently, journalists, gamedevs, and academics have argued that video game stories are at their best when told through random events, procedural generation, and gameplay mechanics.

Thankfully, Amy Hennig believes in writers.

During an interview with *GamesBeat* in 2019, Amy compared video games to *Dungeons & Dragons*, the tabletop role-playing game where a "dungeon master" runs scenarios and stories, and players make decisions and checks to survive, solve mysteries, and interact with the game world. "I'm not saying that we can't have an improvisational quality where players can surprise us," Amy said. "But you still have a dungeon master. There's still somebody guiding the experience. There's still probably some sort of a plan, even if we may deviate from it. That person guiding the experience is trying to guide us to an ending that feels artful and meaningful and resonant, not toward: 'and now we're done.'" If there's one thing to be said for Amy's body of work, it's that every ending she's crafted makes you feel a lot more than "done."

Just a Side Gig

Amy was born in 1956 and, as a kid, spent all of her allowance money on arcade games like *Pong*, *Night Driver*, and, her favorite, *Sea Wolf*. The year she turned thirteen, three things happened that would change her life forever: the first Atari console was released, *Star Wars* debuted in theaters, and *Advanced Dungeons & Dragons*, the role-playing game you might recognize from *Stranger Things* (or from playing it yourself), came out. She told the *Los Angeles Times*, "Our brains were never the same after that." *Star Wars*, in particular, had a profound impact on the kinds of stories Amy wanted to tell: action-adventure romps with iconic characters.

Amy studied English literature at the University of California, Berkeley, and by the time she was twenty-five years old, she was studying film at San Francisco State. At the same time, she took any job that would pay the bills. Then, when at a garage sale, she ran into a friend from high school who had a job recommendation for her. Atari needed a freelance artist for an upcoming video game, *Electrocop*. Amy took the job, and as she created artwork for the game, the idea of interactive stories became more and more interesting to her. She eventually dropped out of film school to pursue a full-time career in games.

Amy's focus shifted from art to design while she was working on *Michael Jordan: Chaos in the Windy City*. The lead designer of the game quit, so Amy stepped in. With that experience on her résumé, she was recruited to work on games as a designer, artist, producer, and writer for multiple studios, including Electronic Arts, Crystal Dynamics, and Eidos Interactive. But her biggest franchise was still ahead of her: the story of a scrappy, clever, charming treasure hunter.

"Don't Let Anybody Get in Your Way"

As both a little girl and as a graduate student, Amy wanted to tell stories like *Indiana Jones* and *Star Wars*. When she joined Naughty Dog in the early 2000s, she got the chance. The studio was trying to figure out what kinds of games they'd make for the PlayStation 3, and Amy helped pitch a funny, epic action-adventure. It was greenlit, and the first *Uncharted* game went into production.

Now Amy's name is synonymous with the *Uncharted* series, the four-game saga of a treasure hunter who travels the world and encounters the supernatural. She was the creative director and a writer on the first three games in the series, meaning she had a lot of the same responsibilities as a movie director. She oversaw gameplay, story, pacing, casting, character designs, environments, animation, and so much more. If a creative decision had to be made, *she made it*. That said, Amy is quick to point out that while she was a major influence on the *Uncharted* series, she wasn't the only one: "We like this idea of there being auteurs, but that's just not reality in film or games," she said onstage during the 2019 DICE Summit, "These things are made by teams of people and groups of people."

Uncharted reimagined what video game stories could do. The series told well-paced, cinematic, playable stories with animated cutscenes and stunning set pieces. A gunfight on a train? Sneaking through a museum at night with your mercenary best friend? Yes, please. Many, if not most, current blockbuster video games look, feel, and play the way they do because of *Uncharted*.

Amy is still one of the few women who have been promoted to "creative director" in games, and as such, she's often asked her thoughts about leadership and sexism in the industry. She's said many times—across interviews, panels, and Q&As—that while many men mentored her, she also had to learn to advocate for herself. "Follow, pursue your dreams," she said to the crowd at the 2019 DICE Summit. "Don't let anybody get in your way. Know your shit. And generally, that means that people can't get their hooks in you if they're trying to pull you down."

Creative Hearts

In March 2019, Amy took the stage at the Game Developers Choice Awards to accept a Lifetime Achievement Award. Like the Industry Icon Award given to Roberta and Ken Williams, the GDCA's Lifetime Achievement Award celebrates someone whose work has meaningfully shaped games, art, and culture. Only nineteen people have won the award since its inception in 2001, and Amy was the first woman to receive the honor. As you can imagine, it is a really, really big deal, and a very important moment for Amy and women game developers. "Well, this is more than a little surreal," she said after taking the podium.

In another creator's hands, it is possible *Uncharted* would never have been made or would have been completely different. The complex blend of film-like story, pacing, settings, and characters—in an interactive space—built a unique, flexible foundation for decades of titles to come, including games like *The Last of Us* (2013), *God of War* (2018), *Marvel's Spider-Man* (2018), *Control* (2019), *Ghost of Tsushima* (2020), and so many more. The *Uncharted* series not only changed how we make games; it changed the types of games people wanted to both buy and make.

Even so, Amy believes the original *Uncharted* would probably not be made today. Why? An eight-hour game with no multiplayer, no open world, and no loot boxes is a really hard sell to most publishers. But innovation is still possible. Amy's quick to point out some of the indie games that have impressed her with their unique storytelling in the last few years, like *What Remains of Edith Finch* (2017), *Journey* (2012) (shout-out to Robin Hunicke on page 25!), and *Florence* (2018). These kinds of games require stories—and their authors, dungeon masters, whatever you want to call them.

In the 2019 *GamesBeat* interview, Amy compared procedurally generated video game stories to paintings done by artificially intelligent machines. "I can be impressed that it made a picture, but there's no soul behind it. I think fundamentally that's what stories are about. You can feel the soul of the people writing it. If they do it well, you feel like they're taking you on a journey, lightly bringing you by the hand. Doesn't a story imply that somebody, with their creative heart, is speaking to you?"

KIM SWIFT

The 2007 blockbuster mega-hit *Portal* started as a student game. Wait, what? In 2005, a group of college students at the DigiPen Institute of Technology released *Narbacular Drop*, a game in which the player creates holes in reality to move around. The team's leader was Kim Swift. When the founder of publisher Valve played *Narbacular Drop*, he offered to hire every one of those students so they could turn their game into a much bigger, more complex title. Kim Swift became a designer at Valve and helped create *Portal* and its 2012 sequel. *Portal* went on to win several Game of the Year awards, was named one of the 100 greatest video games of all time by *Time* magazine in 2012, and was called one of the most influential games of the first decade of the twenty-first century by *Wired*.

CAROL SHAW

"Just another high-strung
prima donna from Atari"

C AROL SHAW IS about the last person you'd call a prima donna, but she is known by another moniker among her former coworkers: superstar. Former Atari programmer Mike Albaugh said of her, "The less publicized superstars, I would have to include Carol Shaw . . . who was simply the best programmer of the 6502 [an early microprocessor used to run games] and probably one of the best programmers period."

But Carol would've been easy to miss in the early years of video games, because the industry had a credits problem. When a video game shipped, the box and credits named the company responsible for making it, but not the developers. When gamedevs started to complain, some of the executives didn't take it well. Ray Kassar, president and CEO of Atari from 1978 to 1983, famously called his employees "high-strung prima donnas" in an interview with *Fortune*. The developers, including Carol, fired back by making T-shirts emblazoned with the slogan JUST ANOTHER HIGH-STRUNG PRIMA DONNA FROM ATARI.

"Why Shouldn't Girls Be Good at Math?"

Carol was born in 1955 in Palo Alto, California, part of the San Francisco Bay. She didn't play video games as a kid because there weren't any, or at least, none that she had access to. Instead, she loved to play with model trains and building sets. In junior and high school, she competed in math competitions and raked in awards. "Of course, people would say, 'Gee, you're good at math—for a girl,'" Carol said in a 2011 interview with *Vintage Computing and Gaming*. "That was kind of annoying. Why shouldn't girls be good at math?"

Carol was already a fan of logic problems and puzzles by the time she reached high school, where she discovered a new hobby: computers. Her math classes included lessons in writing and coding small computer programs. "At first I was somewhat intimidated about going into the computer room," she told *Vintage Computing*, "because it seemed like it was mostly boys using the computers." But she went in anyway, learned her way around basic programming, and found a few text-based games she liked, including a *Star Trek* game.

Carol took three things from her high school computer classes that would come to define her life: computer literacy, attention to detail, and a fondness for games. When she started her freshman year at the University of California at Berkeley, she wasn't sure what she wanted to major in, so she decided to explore her hobbies. She took a few classes in computer science, civil engineering, and programming, and she eventually settled on a degree in electrical engineering and computers. She stayed for an extra year to get a master's degree.

The type of coding Carol learned was very different from how it's done today. In modern game development and coding, bugs are a natural part of the programming process. You write code, and then you "debug" it, combing through to find errors and fix any issues. In the 1970s, it was all done *on paper*. The process back then looked something like this:

Programmers wrote their code out on paper, which would then be punched into "paper tape," then loaded onto the computer to be read. If the code was right, it would appear onscreen. If it was wrong? An error message, and it was time to start over—again, on *paper*. It could be a frustrating process, but Carol had always been patient with puzzles.

After she graduated, she got a job offer from a California company, only five years old at the time: Atari. You probably recognize the name because, today, Atari is one of the biggest game publishers in the world—and Carol is one of the reasons why.

"I Got Paid to Play Games"

Who was the first woman programmer? That question is harder to answer than you might think. It could be Nicole-Reine Lepaute, who in 1757—yes, you read that right—became one of the first "human computers." She worked on calculations to predict when Halley's Comet would return to Earth (it returns approximately every seventy-five years). Or you could say the first woman programmer was Ada Lovelace, who in 1843 published the first algorithm created for a "modern" computer. Or you could answer that the teams of women code breakers in WWII, or NASA coders like Katherine Goble Johnson, Dorothy Vaughan, and Mary Jackson were the first. The point is, women have been programming for a long time.

The field was actually dominated by women in the 1950s and '60s, but as computers started catching on and video games became their own field, more men started to enter the programming space. Along the way, they shut out many of the women who'd been there and discouraged younger women from trying to enter. This attitude became so pervasive that when Carol Shaw started at Atari, CEO Ray Kassar said, "Oh, at last! We have a female game designer. She can do cosmetics color matching and interior decorating cartridges!" To be clear, there is absolutely nothing wrong with wanting to pursue color matching, but assuming that's what someone wants to do or is qualified to do *because of their gender* is not okay. Color matching wasn't Carol's field and certainly not her interest. She was a programmer with an advanced degree in engineering, and that was what she intended to do.

Carol told *Vintage Computers and Gaming* that while Kassar might've jumped to conclusions based on her gender, the other game designers she worked with, thankfully, did not. She also wasn't the only woman at the company. There were two other women working at Atari at the time, Carla Meninsky and Dona Bailey (see Dona's chapter on page 13), though they all worked in different departments. Regardless, all three were instrumental in building the first generation of Atari games and consoles.

One of those early projects was the game *Polo*, created in 1978. Warner Communications, the owner of Ralph Lauren, had recently purchased Atari and wanted a game to tie in with a polo-centric cologne. Okay, that sentence was a lot, let's back up. Ralph Lauren's logo is a guy playing polo, the sport where you hit things with a big mallet while you ride horseback. Ralph Lauren also sells cologne. To make people want to buy that cologne, Warner decided to make a video game based on the sport. Sure, why not? It's unclear how Warner intended to use the game: As a gift to people who bought lots of cologne? A marketing campaign lining the shelves of computer stores? Impossible to say. Carol was on the team that created the cartridges and handwritten instructions on how to play the game. When they finished, the game was sent to New York so the folks at Warner could review it . . . and the Atari team *never* heard from them *again*. The game didn't ship, but history buffs have studied prototypes and art for it. In 2017, curator Shannon Symonds from The Strong National Museum of Play called *Polo* "perhaps the first documented game designed and programmed by a woman."

After *Polo*, Carol worked on four more games and helped fix or improve many more. During her time, her official title was "microprocessor software engineer," though today she'd probably be called a designer or a gameplay programmer. Even that title is a little misleading, because the term "designer" encompasses different responsibilities at different companies. For Carol, being an Atari engineer meant doing *everything.* "In those days, one person would do the entire game: the design, the programming, the graphics, and sound," she told *Vintage Computing and Gaming.* "Then you'd get feedback from the other designers, but basically one person did the whole thing." As mentioned in Dona's chapter, sometimes engineers worked together on projects, but most of the time, making games meant flying solo.

Carol settled into her job and kept making lots of cool games at Atari. That sounds like a happily ever after, right? Not quite. After two years and four games, Carol left Atari, and she joined Activision in 1982. That same year, she created and released one of the first games to be banned by an entire nation.

Wait, what?

CARLA MENINSKY

Carla Meninsky was, alongside Carol Shaw and Dona Bailey, one of the first three women to work at Atari as an engineer. She helped develop their video game cartridges, which are the little blocks of plastic you'd stick into a console to play a game in the days before discs and digital downloads. Growing up, Carla had many interests, from programming to neuropsychology to animation. She eventually studied psychology at Stanford University, but she learned enough programming to be hired at Atari. Later, she went to work for Electronic Arts and eventually started her own programming company. Working in video games helped her develop an interest in law that covers creative properties, and she is currently a lawyer working in the field of intellectual property law.

So Good, We Banned It

The banned game in question was *River Raid*, one of the first shooter games ever made, and Carol was its designer. In the game, you control an airplane cruising above a river.

Your task is to shoot down enemy tankers and other targets for points. The game was a hit with gamers and the community, selling 1 million copies and winning awards like "best computer action game" and "best action game." It would go on to inspire games like *Raiden*, one of the most popular arcade shooters ever made, and *TwinBee*, an early variant of the "cute 'em up" genre. (If you guessed that "cute 'em up" is a shooter with cute graphics, *ding ding ding*, you win!)

But back to the banned games list. The German Federal Department for Media Harmful to Young Persons, or Bundesprüfstelle für jugendgefährdende Medien in German, created a list of media it thought might have a bad influence on children. *River Raid* was the first video game to be included. Though that stung, there's a silver lining to the story: it meant that video games were starting to draw notice on a wider pop culture scale. And the story does have a happy ending: in 2002, the department admitted that *River Raid* never should have made the list.

SIDE QUEST — BETTY RYAN TYLKO AND CAROL RYAN THOMAS

Two sisters, two jobs, one company. Betty Ryan Tylko was the first woman to be hired as a programmer at General Computer Corporation, also known as GCC, a company that turned arcade games into home console games. Her sister, Carol Ryan Thomas, joined GCC not long after as a tester and debugger. Both were among the first women gamedevs in the United States. In the times when Carol had to stick up for herself and her place in the industry, she was quick to name Betty as her inspiration. "Seeing my sister Betty get into Harvard at a time when computer science wasn't even a major, and seeing her go through everything she had to go through in a field that was really male-dominated, I guess I felt like I'd let her down if I let somebody walk all over me."

Industry Icon

In 2017, Carol took the stage at The Game Awards—basically, the Oscars of video games. She hadn't made a game in more than thirty years, but when she was handed a tall chromatic trophy, the crowd went wild. Carol held her trophy in one hand and a slip of yellow paper in the other. The paper trembled as she spoke to the crowd of thousands, but her voice never wavered. She thanked her parents, wishing her father had lived to see this and smiling at how proud her mother was. She thanked her former coworkers and her husband, who grinned proudly from the audience. His eyebrows shot up in surprise when the crowd applauded him. Then Carol said, "Video games have really progressed since I was working on them thirty-five years ago. The first thing I noticed is, the graphics have really gotten a lot better." She laughed along with the audience. "But the classic games are still fun to play," she added, and the crowd erupted into whoops and applause.

Her reaction to being named an Industry Icon at The Game Awards, the highest award given to an individual game developer, was a humble thanks and a reflection on how much games have changed since she made them. Carol Shaw is about as far from a prima donna as you can get, but seriously, she has every right to be celebrated and seen as the iconic creator that she is.

MABEL ADDIS MERGARDT

The first person to write a video game

SK SOMEONE WHAT the first video game was, and you'll probably get a variety of answers ranging from "uhh" to "huh?" Once that's out of the way, they may brighten and say, "*Pong*!" Or, if they're one of those people who stays up past midnight scrolling Wikipedia, "*Spacewar!*" However, they're both wrong, and since you're reading this book, you'll know the answer and get to be super smug about it. The answer is *Tennis for Two*, which, to be fair, is an early version of *Pong*, or OXO, a game programmed at Cambridge in 1952. Wedged in right next to them is a game very few people have heard of, called *The Sumerian Game*, and it was the first video game *with a story*. That story was written by a teacher with a love for theater named Mabel Addis Mergardt, video games' first writer. *Ever.*

Teaching Through Play

So you already know that Mabel wasn't a programmer. She didn't study art, engineering, animation, or even writing. She didn't grow up with computers, and she'd never played a video game when she pitched an idea for one (because there were none for her to play). She was born on May 21, 1912, a month before the *Titanic* sank and two years before World War I began. If you've watched *Downton Abbey*, then you have a pretty good picture of the era in which Mabel was born.

In 1929, Mabel graduated as the valedictorian of Brewster High School in Brewster, New York. She studied ancient history and psychology at Barnard College, graduating in 1933, before attending Columbia University in New York City for a master's degree in teaching. Mabel graduated from college forty years before the first home computers were mass produced, fifty-five years before the World Wide Web (the early internet) was invented. When she started teaching, it was in a one-room schoolhouse.

There were many things Mabel didn't have access to, like computers or even the programming-on-paper of later game designers like Carol Shaw (page 56) and Elonka Dunin (page 131). What she had plenty of was curiosity. In addition to teaching, she co-authored two history books about towns in New York: *Katonah: A History of a New York Village* and *Brewster Throughout the Years*. She wrote articles, started an oral history collection, and served on multiple committees. She loved to write plays for her students and used them as teaching tools to make her lessons interactive.

All the foundations of Mabel's video game, *The Sumerian Game*, can be found in these roots. She studied ancient history before writing a game about an ancient society, and she wrote plays intended to teach. Many academics and game scholars have compared games to theater because they share many elements, like interactivity, the audience's suspension of disbelief, and the "magic circle" of the game or stage that lets you step into another world with new rules. It's no wonder, then, that when IBM launched a program to use computers and stories to teach kids, Mabel Addis was one of the people they reached out to for help.

The Ruler of Lagash

To play *The Sumerian Game*, you didn't sit in front of a monitor or TV. Instead, you sat in front of a printer. An IBM 1050 terminal, to be exact, which was connected to a mainframe computer—remember, personal computers weren't a thing yet—and a slide projector. When you started the game, an audio tape played and you moved the slides along. It introduced you to the world and goals of *The Sumerian Game*, and it was the first unskippable cutscene in a video game.

These instructions are preserved in manuals, but you can't play *The Sumerian Game* anymore: copies and methods to play it no longer exist. Even so, the projector slides and printouts are on display at The Strong National Museum of Play in Rochester, New York, and its influence can still be felt in many modern video games. *The Sumerian Game* made resource management and city-building interesting by adding a story and characters that players cared about. This idea would go on to inspire popular games like *SimCity* and *Civilization*, and it all happened because of Mabel.

So, back to IBM. The company put out the call to school districts and boards of education, looking for teachers to help pitch and create educational games. Mabel was among the teachers who volunteered to work on the project, and for five years, she spent her summers—when she wasn't teaching—working on *The Sumerian Game*.

The game began as a prototype made by Bruse Moncreiff, an IBM employee. He'd created an economic model meant to teach basic resource management. It was loosely based on the board game *Monopoly*, and Mabel thought the prototype had potential. She told Bruse what she wanted to add: a story, characters, and a setting that made kids want to learn about and manage the economy and resources. Bruse agreed, and the two became a team.

First, they wanted to give the game a grounded setting. They agreed it should be a pre-Greek civilization because these are some of the most influential societies ever to exist, yet they're rarely taught in American public-school curriculums. Bruse and Mabel landed on Mesopotamia as their game's setting. IBM gave them the greenlight and assigned them a programmer, William McKay, and production on *The Sumerian Game* began.

The basics were already in place from Moncreiff's early prototype, but Mabel made the numbers and simulations *mean* something. She decided the player would play as three different characters, successive rulers of the city of Lagash. She set the year, 3500 BC. She took Bruse's idea of playing the game in rounds and described them as "seasons." She named the resources things like population and grain. If you were winning the game, your population and harvest numbers went up. Random disasters could hit, like floods and fires, impacting your numbers and requiring quick thinking. Mabel turned columns of numbers into a story with meaning and consequences.

Today, this is often called a "narrative wrapper," the story that *wraps* around the gameplay to give the player an emotional investment in what happens. Long before professional video game writers would coin the term "narrative wrapper," Mabel understood why one was necessary. She realized, through her own experience as a playwright and teacher, that students were more than eager to learn through play—they just needed a good story to pull them through.

Anyone who has studied education and psychology knows that play has a major role in how people develop and learn. It's not just humans, either. Have you ever watched a puppy or kitten play with a ball or length of string? If not, close this book right now, and go watch a few videos on the internet. Okay, are you back? Is your soul nourished? Cool. The point is, animals play when they're young, and so do humans, but why? The Canadian Council on Learning explains it this way: "Play nourishes every aspect of children's development— it forms the foundation of intellectual, social, physical, and emotional skills necessary for success in school and in life. Play paves the way for learning."

As a teacher, Mabel knew this, but no one had applied the idea to computers, let alone computer games. No one had thought to sit a child in front of a computer, tell them a story, and present them with a problem. No one except Mabel. Her creativity had become intertwined with computer programming to teach kids about history and basic economics. The question now was: Would it work, and would kids enjoy it?

Let's Try That Again

Nope. Not at first, anyway.

The year was 1966, and *The Sumerian Game* needed heavy revisions. Mabel had spent every summer for the last three years working on the game, but when IBM brought in thirty students to test it, it didn't go well. The game was too long. The numbers were confusing. The instructions were unclear. It's a moment that's happened at least once (speaking from my experience, *way more than once*) to every gamedev: players say the game isn't fun, or it's confusing, or maybe it's just boring. So, now what?

Revisions. Mabel reworked the scripts. She, Bruse, and William shortened the game and removed some mechanics so players were less overwhelmed. Mabel decreased the number of messages that told the player how they were doing, to make them less repetitive. The team added graphs and charts to serve as a kind of progress map. And they added voice acting, possibly the first video game to ever do so, though it wasn't *in* the game itself: they added the tape recorder the player could listen to. On the tape was a "discussion" among the cabinet of advisors in Lagash, which described the problems the player would face. This had previously been lines of text, but allowing students to listen helped them to absorb the story before they started making decisions in the game.

1967 rolled around, and it was time to show the revised game to kids. This time, the results were good: the students enjoyed the story and retained what they'd learned about economic management and ancient history. *The Sumerian Game* could both entertain and teach, and IBM's idea that computers could be used as learning devices was confirmed.

So, once again, the question became: Now what?

LIZZIE MAGIE

We all know the money-making, property-buying game *Monopoly*: it takes several hours to play, features brightly colored paper, and lets you move around the board as a tiny metal thimble or car. What you might not know is the story of the woman behind the game, Lizzie Magie. She, like Mabel Addis Mergardt, created a game with the intent to teach.

When Lizzie Magie invented the game in 1903, she didn't name it *Monopoly*. She called it *The Landlord's Game*. She meant it to be a commentary on the way rich people hoarded land and public resources, creating monopolies that harmed others. Her friends loved the game, so a year after she created it, Lizzie patented *The Landlord's Game*, sold it, and distributed it. It swept like wildfire across the northeastern United States, especially among middle-class families, Quakers, and students at Harvard, Yale, and Columbia. Lizzie had made more than a game; she'd made a piece of art with a firm political stance.

However, thirty years after she invented *The Landlord's Game*, a man claimed *he'd* invented a totally separate, not-at-all-the-same game called *Monopoly* in his basement. Parker Brothers, a growing toy company, bought the idea from him and credited him for the game's design. Lizzie protested, pointing out the many similarities between her game and his. While his version de-emphasized the message against monopolies, the rest of the design was incredibly close. Parker Brothers agreed to publish two other games created by Lizzie, but they refused to give her credit for *Monopoly*. Yuck.

So, let's set the record straight: Lizzie Magie invented *The Landlord's Game*, and a modified version of it, *Monopoly*, became one of the most popular board games of all time. Now you know.

The Sumerian Legacy

The Sumerian Game, like so many early video games, pushed against the technological limits of its time. Home computers were still ten years away from being invented, so there was no way to widely distribute it to schools or homes. Unfortunately, the project ran out of funding.

After the money was gone, *The Sumerian Game* became IBM's property and disappeared into its archives. However, it wasn't forgotten. In 1966, both *Time* and *Life* magazines wrote about the game and its impact on computers and learning. Furthermore, the game had gained traction among other programmers, including a student at John Hopkins and an employee at Digital Equipment Corporation. They began playing with the code and seeing what they could create, making them among the first active modding communities in video games.

As for Mabel, *The Sumerian Game* was her first and last game. Despite being the first game writer and the first woman game designer, she hasn't been included in many lists exploring the achievements of women in games, honored in industry events, or featured prominently in museums. But she was still the first, and she understood the importance of storytelling in play long before the video game industry would. Her influence had an impact on the way we understand computers, learning, and storytelling. So the next time you pick up a controller, take a moment to remember and thank Mabel.

CHRISTY MARX

Ever heard of the *Teenage Mutant Ninja Turtles*? Of course you have. What you probably don't know is that Christy Marx, one of the TV show's writers, also has an extensive background in video games. Her first video game, *Conquests of Camelot*, shipped in 1990, and she was a writer for its 1991 sequel, *Conquests of the Longbow*. She joined Zynga, an American video game developer, in 2011 and worked there for six years. Meanwhile, she wrote four history books on topics ranging from the Great Chicago Fire of 1871 to a history of Jet Li. Like Mabel Addis Mergardt, Christy understands how to tell a story that both educates and entertains, and she's applied that to television, games, books, and comics for more than thirty years.

DANIELLE
BUNTEN BERRY

The programmer who refused to sit
in front of a computer alone

THERE ARE A lot of game developers on Twitter. We talk about our games, our workplaces, and our dream projects. We share fanart, insights, and behind-the-scenes fun facts. We become friends with each other and set up coffee or game dates. We trot out our sometimes silly, sometimes deadpan humor, and share our happiness as well as our anger and weariness. If Twitter had been around when Danielle Bunten Berry was making games, she would've fit right in.

In the early 2000s, Danielle created and operated her own website, AntiClockwise.com, where she talked about everything from game design to her children to her experiences as a transgender woman. She wrote openly and with a dry sense of humor about both her joys and regrets. "I remember a time when I was walking at the mall with a gay friend and watching all the 'normal' families," she wrote. "I told him in a sad and regretful tone how I'll never be normal again. He responded, 'You've got it wrong . . . you need to say,' with an exultant tone he shouted, 'I'll never be normal again!' It turns out he was right: escaping the 'normal' is what all of us need to do to become who we really are!"

A Lifelong Gamer

Like many of the women in this book, Danielle started playing games when she was a child. For her, games were a social exercise, meant to be enjoyed by groups rather than individuals plunked down in front of a board, deck, or computer. "When I was a kid, the only times my family spent together that weren't totally dysfunctional were when we were playing games," she told James Hague for his 1997 book *Halcyon Days: Interviews with Classic Computer and Video Game Programmers*. "Consequently, I believe games are a wonderful way to socialize. Also," she added with a touch of the irreverent, self-deprecating sense of humor she became known for, "I'm a control freak and love making rules for other people to follow." An important side note: Danielle and Anne Westfall (find her "Side Quest" on page 4!) were the only women interviewed for the book.

Danielle was born in 1949, the oldest of six kids, and when she was just six years old, her family moved to Little Rock, Arkansas—Dona Bailey's hometown (page 13), and apparently a great starting spot for future rock-star game developers. Danielle's family didn't have much money when she was growing up, so to help pay the bills, she worked a part-time job at the local drugstore and became a Scoutmaster in the Boy Scouts of America. Later, when she was twenty-two years old and studying at the University of Arkansas, she opened her own bicycle shop, the Highroller Cyclerie, which is just about the coolest name one could give a bike shop.

After she graduated college with a degree in industrial engineering, Danielle got a job with the National Science Foundation, which she called "the closest thing to building games I could find." She worked in urban planning for a while before she decided to try *actually* making games for a living. The result of that decision was *Wheeler Dealers*, a real-time multi-player auction game for the Apple II computer. In 1978, she sold the game to a Canadian software company, Speakeasy Software, and the game shipped the same year.

In those days, American computer games were sold in little baggies and cost around $15. However, *Wheeler Dealers* required a custom controller to play, which bumped up its price to $35, so the game sold only fifty copies. Though it wasn't commercially successful, *Wheeler Dealers* was crucial to Danielle's career because it was her first time tinkering with multiplayer, the genre she would come to define in its earliest days.

After *Wheeler Dealers*, Danielle made three more games in three years before cofounding a company, Ozark Softscape, in Little Rock with her brother and two other devs. Simultaneously, her games were starting to draw attention from both gamers and other developers. One person in particular had just founded his own game start-up, and he wanted Danielle to create unique games for it. His name? Trip Hawkins. His little company? Electronic Arts.

JAMIE FENTON

From the time she was small, Jamie Fenton loved the predictable nature of computers. Jamie spent a lot of her time with them, which led to a career in video games. In 1975, she was hired to redesign pinball machines with a new microprocessor, and she went on to program the 1981 arcade game *Gorf*, which you might recognize from its cameo in *Stranger Things*.

Today, Jamie's an active voice in the transgender and video game communities. When someone asked her if men have more "technical brains," she answered, "Well, I've always had a female brain. Computers were a safe place for me to go, because they never picked on me, and they were very predictable."

Time Enough for M.U.L.E.

A misconception many people have about programmers is that they're all introverts: quiet, shy, and glued to their computers. Not Danielle. Witty, extroverted, and interested in how computers could connect people to one another, she broke just about every preconception people might have about her. In her interview for *Halcyon Days*, she quipped, "Damn, I can sound pretty articulate for an Arkie"—someone from Arkansas—"don't ya think?" No surprise, then, that she was also interested in breaking the preconceptions people had about games—namely, that they needed to be single-player experiences.

Imagine this: A blue-and-purple ship streaks across the screen and it deposits you and three friends on the surface of an alien planet called Irata. The four of you run until blocks of numbers appear; it's a list of your resources, including land, money, and goods. Then, the ship leaves. It will be back in six months, so you need to work together to keep the colony alive—while also working against each other to amass the most wealth for yourself. The game, *M.U.L.E.*, is a balance of self-interest and survival, with random events like sunspots and space pirates to keep you on guard.

To begin, Danielle drew inspiration from several sources. The first was her own game, *Wheeler Dealers*. Using it as a baseline, she wanted to create a more seamless and engaging multiplayer system—without the need for a custom controller. Another inspiration was the 1973 science fiction novel *Time Enough for Love*, in which people travel to other planets and colonize them with old-fashioned tools. Danielle used the spacefaring survival problem as the narrative wrapper (we introduced this term in Mabel Addis Mergardt's chapter on page 62) in *M.U.L.E.*, giving meaning to the game's economics and resources challenges. Finally, like Amy Hennig (page 52), Danielle was inspired by *Star Wars*. The titular M.U.L.E., aka the Multiple Use Labor Element, is a machine the player uses to harvest resources on their land. Part of the game's strategy is to build more M.U.L.E.s and increase opportunities to harvest resources. These elements, combined with gameplay that focused on resource gathering, survival, random events, and competition, resulted in a spacefaring multiplayer adventure ready to ship in 1983.

M.U.L.E. was one of the first games produced by Electronic Arts, but initially, Trip Hawkins didn't want Danielle to create a new game at all. He'd wanted to buy the rights to *Cartels & Cutthroats*, a game Danielle and her team had already shipped in 1981. The game's original publisher, Strategic Simulations, wouldn't sell, so Danielle promised Trip she could make a new game that would be *even better*. It was a risk, but Danielle convinced Trip it was one worth taking.

Trip's gamble on a new game—and on Danielle—paid off. Though *M.U.L.E.* sold only 30,000 copies, it did so on the Atari 800 console, which Atari stopped making within a few months of *M.U.L.E.*'s release. Selling 30,000 copies in just a few months meant the game was a critical success. Plus, critics *adored it*. They praised the strategy, the joystick, and the innovative gameplay. *M.U.L.E.* won numerous awards and honors, including becoming one of the first games in *Computer Game World*'s Hall of Fame, a list of the games rated most highly by the magazine's readers. In 2004, *GameSpot* named *M.U.L.E.* one of the greatest games of all time, and outlets like *PC World* and *1Up.com* did the same.

During the interview for *Halcyon Days*, James asked Danielle when she realized *M.U.L.E.* was "special." She admitted that even after the game had made her and Electronic Arts famous, she still wasn't sure if the game was special. "During development, I get more and more excited about the game as I design solutions to problems," she said. "However, if I go back and play the game after a year or so, I'm inevitably depressed by the problems I see in the design.

"But good or bad, it's my baby," she added, "and I'm glad I built it."

All That Glitters Is Seven Cities

It would have been easy for Danielle to sit back and enjoy *M.U.L.E.*'s success. Easy, but not in character. This was a woman who opened a bicycle shop while studying engineering, who worked part-time at a drugstore and babysat many younger siblings while she was just a child. Sitting still was not in her nature. Not long after *M.U.L.E.* debuted, Danielle and her Ozark team went on a trip to—where else?—the Ozark Mountains, in the middle of the United States, to start brainstorming their next game. Danielle called it *Civilization*.

Now wait a darn minute, you might be thinking. Civilization *was made by Sid Meier (and a whole bunch of other people). His name is on the box! Sid Meier's* Civilization! And you're right. The game you are thinking of wouldn't come out for another eight years, helmed by Mr. Sid Meier himself. During their retreat, Danielle pitched a similar idea, which she also called *Civilization*, but no one at Ozark was excited about it. Instead, the team decided to make an exploration game. The inspiration for this one hit a little closer to home for Danielle. She'd recently gone on a backpacking trip in Arkansas, and she got lost. Though she knew she was never more than a day away from a major road, the feeling of being alone and unsure in the wilderness lodged inside her. It provided the perfect feeling to chase in her next game.

The Seven Cities of Gold launched a year after *M.U.L.E.* and was one of the first in a genre that had barely begun to be defined: open world. Open world means the player is dropped onto a map that they can explore at their leisure, interacting with different activities and areas whenever they want to, rather than being pulled through a linear story or directed to choose from a list of missions. Open-world games usually have a main goal or storyline, but it's up to the player when and where to interact with it, and they can skip it altogether if they want to. I say this as someone who has logged more than three hundred hours in *The Elder Scrolls: Skyrim* but never completed the main storyline (I will, someday! I swear!). It was also Danielle's first single-player game, as the multiplayer angle was scrapped during development.

In *Seven Cities*, the player is a Spanish colonizer whose aim is to find gold, use it to win the Spanish court's favor, and, along the way, discovers the hidden seven cities of gold. Part of the gameplay centers around how you treat the Indigenous peoples who live there, as allies or enemies, something Danielle spoke about in a 1985 interview with *Antic*. "The peaceful approach really works best. I have not used a totally depraved approach and won. You've got to have some friends somewhere." If the player chooses a violent approach, eventually a message from the king will appear, telling them to stop treating people so badly. But, simultaneously, to keep sending gold to Spain. "This double standard is straight out of history," Danielle added.

When Danielle shipped *M.U.L.E.*, she was still fairly new to the games industry, and no one expected a work of genius. After *M.U.L.E.*, the gaming community turned a spotlight on Danielle and wondered if she could recreate her success. The answer was *yes*, Danielle could create more than one good game. When *Seven Cities* shipped in 1984, critics called it "riveting" and "exceptional." It became Danielle's bestselling game at more than 100,000 copies sold.

By 1985, Danielle had released multiple award-winning games and helped shape the beginnings of two important game genres: multiplayer and open world. She'd earned her place as one of the most influential game developers of all time, but now she wanted some time away from computers. At the 1990 Game Developers Conference, Danielle gave the keynote address and famously said, "No one ever said on their deathbed, 'Gee, I wish I had spent more time alone with my computer.'"

To Become Who We Really Are

Danielle passed away from lung cancer in 1998, but people continue to study and write about her work to this day. After combing through the archives at The Strong Museum, professor and historian Whitney Pow wrote about Danielle for *ROMchip*, a games history journal, in 2019. Reflecting on her career and personality, Whitney wrote of her like someone reflecting on an old friend. "I recently heard Bunten's voice for the first time in a digitized cassette recording of a talk she gave at the Computer Game Developers Conference (now known as GDC) in 1998. In it, she is full of actions and verbs, and she moves me: her voice is hoarse; she takes short breaths; her talk is interspersed with coughs. She has a markedly Southern accent. She occasionally uses the word 'ain't.' She talks candidly about her pronoun change. She makes jokes to Sid Meier and other game developer friends in the audience."

Since then, Danielle has been lionized by the games industry. In 2000, Will Wright dedicated *The Sims* to Danielle's memory. In 2007, Sid Meier (yes, the guy mentioned above—his name is on *Civilization*'s box!) inducted Danielle into the Academy of Interactive Arts & Sciences Hall of Fame. Her influence lives on, and her writing, speeches, and source codes can still be found online today. Much of her work is housed in The Strong National Museum of Play, and Danielle's last GDC talk in 1998, "Do Online Games Still Suck?" is available in the GDC Vault, an online repository of past Game Developers Conference talks and panels.

What Danielle left behind was a family she loved—you can see that in her many blogposts—as well as a legacy of challenging what games could and should be. "I still believe we're in the early days of this industry and have a lot to discover and invent," Danielle said in her interview for *Halcyon Days*. "Literature, anthropology, and even dance have a good deal more to teach designers about human drives and abilities than the technologists on either end of California, who know silicon and celluloid but not much else."

For Danielle, creating video games was a chance to gather a family around a computer, as her own family had once gathered around a table to play board games. It's impossible to know how many friends and families she brought together, but obvious that her life touched and connected thousands of people.

CORRINNE YU

The most influential engineer you haven't heard of . . . yet

W HEN APPLE DONATED a bunch of computers to a junior high school in California, everyone stared at them "like they were doorstops." It was the 1980s, and no one was quite sure what to do with them. No one except Corrinne Yu. She loved to take apart electronics and put them back together again, so her school asked if she could use any of the donated computers. She said yes, and that's how Corrinne— the engineer who would one day program the engines that powered games like *Halo* and *Borderlands*—began teaching herself to code.

Just a Hobby

Corrinne was born in Hong Kong, China, and moved to California with her family when she was still a little girl. She was fluent in Cantonese and learned English after she came to the United States. To this day, she does much of her arithmetic in Cantonese.

After she taught herself to code with her school's donated computers, the school offered her a job creating automated programs that could do things like track grades. Corrinne pulled it off, and she saved the money—from her first programming job!—to buy her own Apple II computer. With it, she started making games for her friends and brothers. Corrinne later described making games as figuring out how complex pieces fit together to make something beautiful. The first beautiful something she made was a top-down sports game based on American football. Then, she built a 3D dungeon as a companion to a tabletop *Dungeons & Dragons* campaign. "It wasn't until much later that I found out other people and even companies made games," she told *Edge* magazine in 2014. "It never occurred to me before then." Game development and even programming weren't on Corrinne's radar when she decided to go to college. She didn't realize programming could be an actual career path because she thought it was too much *fun*. Instead, she studied electrical engineering at California State Polytechnic University.

Corrinne continued programming on the side, as a hobby, and after she graduated, it became her first full-time job. She was hired as a programmer on NASA's Space Shuttle program at Rockwell International California. Despite her rather serious job, or maybe because of it, Corrinne didn't stop making games in her spare time. She programmed them as a way to relax, cure boredom, or just take a break from worrying about the space shuttle. She wasn't trying to sell them, but she showed them to a few friends. Since many of her friends also worked in programming and engineering, word spread about Corrinne's interest in games and her talent for making them. Gamedevs started trying to recruit Corrinne to come work for them.

It wasn't an easy choice. Game development is never a steady career path, thanks to things like layoffs and studio closures, and in the 1990s, it was even less so. Corrinne wanted to spend her career creating things of lasting value and worth. It wasn't clear to her back then how long games would stick around.

"I had to go through a lot of internal rationalizations to justify my decision," Corrinne told *Edge* in 2014. "But now I feel that I've seen the impact games have had in the world, I don't feel conflicted anymore. Millions of people enjoy playing things that I helped make. Perhaps it makes them happier people, and they improve the world."

SIDE QUEST

XIAOYUAN TU

Of all the exciting things about the Nintendo Wii, high on the list was the MotionPlus controller. For the first time, players could hold, wave, and interact with the controller, and the console would register those actions even if it wasn't plugged into anything. Xiaoyuan Tu is one of the people behind those very cool controllers. She's a scientist who specializes in helping machines learn and think. Without her technology and research, we never would've been able to play *Wii Sports – Bowling*, and the world would be worse for it.

Complex Pieces Fitting Together

Once Corrinne made the jump to video games, she stayed in the industry for more than twenty years. She solved problems others had only created workarounds for. For example, while working at Gearbox Software, she modified the Unreal Engine 3 to improve physics, lighting, and shadows. Unreal Engine 3 powers more than a hundred Xbox 360 and PlayStation 3 games, including *Batman: Arkham City*, all three *Mass Effect* games, *DmC: Devil May Cry*, *Dishonored*, *Bioshock Infinite*, and *Mortal Kombat X* and *11*. "By making things less static and more reactive to what the player does, then I am contributing to the narrative that games are trying to tell, and the emotional resonance," she told *Edge*.

After working at Gearbox, Corrinne joined another studio, 343 Industries, and worked on the *Halo* franchise. The technology and algorithms she invented for *Halo 4*'s lighting were so original and groundbreaking, Microsoft applied for a software patent so other studios couldn't replicate it without credit. Microsoft also named Corrinne a technical lead, someone who oversees teams of software developers and engineers, and she was the first woman at Microsoft to hold the job.

It would be an oversimplification to say, "Corrinne made the graphics in *Halo* better," because her work changed how games are made. Once she figured out how to improve lighting and animation in *Halo* and other games, it set an industry standard for quality. Corrinne wanted to make games that made people think, and she viewed the technology she was creating—making games more immersive, fluid, and artistic—as a means to that end. She made the math work so creativity wouldn't be limited by the technology. Given her success on some of the most popular games ever made, it's no surprise that in 2009, the Game Developers Conference awarded Corrinne Best in Engineering in the *world*.

Not that her role came without difficulties. Though she was primarily a programmer and technology director, Corrinne wanted to contribute more than that. She saw herself as a game developer, but many of the people she worked with assumed her interests were limited to coding. "People see limitations when they think of graphical engineers," she told *Edge*. "They don't think we have a creative inclination or talent. You're dismissed as a math nerd."

The desire to contribute to games' narrative and creative direction led Corrinne to Naughty Dog, the studio behind the *Uncharted* and *The Last of Us* series (and where Amy Hennig, page 52, worked for so long). But as the *Uncharted* series was coming to an end, so was Corrinne's time in the games industry.

The Next Problem

In 2014, Corrinne left Naughty Dog and game development altogether. She took a job working on drones for Amazon, and since then has worked for General Motors and Facebook. While Corrinne might have moved on from games, the technological marvels she created have had a lasting impact on how games look, feel, and play.

Over the course of her career, Corrinne has won awards in everything from nuclear physics to engineering, earned patents for her innovations, and started companies and led technology departments. In short, there are very few obstacles Corrinne didn't find a way to overcome.

And through it all, she never stopped making small games for her friends. While working as a lead programmer at Naughty Dog, Corrinne also created iOS games on the side. Why? Because, for Corrinne, programming and game development aren't just jobs; they're a chance to be creative.

Today, Corrinne encourages girls to pursue their love of math and technology and not let anyone—or any fear—stop them. In an interview with *Girl Gamer*, she described game programming as a "wonderful career" that bridges "hardware design, completion-ist world simulation, exploration of esoteric math, and many intellectually rewarding fields." Math nerds who love GPU shaders and vectorized arithmetic; AI specialists who want to tweak weapons and vehicle velocity; theoretical mathematicians: there's a place for all of them in games.

REBECCA HEINEMAN

First national video game tournament champion

F OR MOST OF Rebecca's career, no one called her by her name; they called her "Burger." The reason why remained a mystery for many years, but in 2010, Rebecca Heineman unveiled the mystery in an interview with *Gamasutra*.

The story goes like this: The year was 1983, and Rebecca and three other developers had just founded Interplay Productions, the studio that would go on to create the *Fallout* series. Though Interplay would eventually become a heavy hitter, in 1983 its cofounders were broke. The three had come from Boone Corporation, a studio that folded while they were all working there. Even before Boone went out of business, Rebecca had made just $12,000 a year working there—which wasn't much even in 1983. Her life after cofounding Interplay boiled down to sleeping, working, and finding a few minutes in between those two to eat. Her solution to a lack of time and money? Hamburger Stand, which sold 29-cent hamburgers. A bag of twenty hamburgers cost her $6, so she bought a giant bag and socked away the burgers in a drawer in her desk. No mini fridge, no coolers, just a drawer full of burgers. When she got hungry, she grabbed a burger. No cooking required, and it was affordable on a gamedev's start-up salary. *Perfect*.

Well, not quite. Rebecca had an office mate who pushed her to eat healthier. She argued that she was too busy working to worry about things like *vegetables*. One day, after pulling an all-nighter, Rebecca looked up and realized it was 3 p.m. and that she hadn't eaten since the day before. That meant one thing: burger time. She popped open her desk, grabbed her dinner/breakfast/lunch burger, and started to eat. Her office mate looked at her, realized where she'd gotten the burger, and mentally tabulated how long it had probably been sitting there. He promptly stood up, ran away, and got sick. The story spread through Interplay, and before long, Rebecca was known as "Burger."

Today, "Burger" is part of her website, her Twitter handle, and in multiple headlines about her. It also, for many years, was the name that most accurately described her. "Later on, unbeknownst to anybody, I had an issue with the name I was given at birth," she told *Gamasutra*. "So, I would rather be called Burger than by that birth name. 'Just call me Burger.' For the next twenty years, that was my name. Everybody called me Burger. Now my name is Becky. I finally shed the name Burger."

Before She Was Burger

Becky fell in love with games as a kid growing up in Whittier, California, a town of dusty brown hills half an hour east of Los Angeles. She spent most of her time playing video games with her friend, Tom. She copied game cartridges Tom owned so she could play on her Atari 2600 or Apple II, effectively designing her own "devkit," the version of consoles gamedevs use to make games.

On October 11, 1980, when Becky was still a teenager, the Los Angeles Atari 2600 *Space Invaders* regional was held at the Topanga Canyon Plaza, a mall not far from where Tom and Becky lived. Tom persuaded her to compete. She didn't think she had any chance of doing well, but she agreed to go along with it. They went to the mall, and Becky started to play. She didn't find it particularly challenging.

"I was talking with the judge because I had nothing better to do," Becky recalled in the *Gamasutra* interview thirty years later. I was like, 'Oh, I just lost a base,' and play, play, play, play, and another hour would go by. Base, play, play, play. 'What's my score?' And he said, 'You've got like 83 thousand six hundred points.' And of course, my reply was, 'Is that good?'" It wasn't just *good*; it was *the best* in Los Angeles. Becky had won the tournament, and she was going to the national competition in New York City.

Upon arriving at nationals, it was apparent to Becky that she'd made it big-time. Each contestant wore a T-shirt with their city emblazoned across it—for Becky, that meant LOS ANGELES in big letters. They were each set up with their own TV and console. Judges patrolled behind them, watching their scores climb and making sure they couldn't cheat. Games journalists watched and took notes.

The competition took almost two hours, and when it was finally time to announce the scores, Becky had no idea how she'd done. She'd been too focused on her own game to watch anyone else. "I just reached over and yanked out the cartridge," she told *Gamasutra*, "and said, 'That's it! I'm done with this game!'"

The winners were announced by city, from lowest score to highest. The highest scorer would be the first video game tournament champion—ever. Becky waited and listened. She didn't expect to win, but she hoped she'd done well enough to come in second place, since the second-place prize was an Atari 800 computer.

Chicago, they called first. Texas. San Francisco. New York. *Los Angeles.*

How to Win at Video Games

Not long after Rebecca was crowned the best *Space Invaders* player in America, people wanted her to write articles on how to, well, be the best *Space Invaders* player in America. So she wrote articles for *Electronic Games Magazine* and gave advice in two books, *How to Master the Video Games* and *How to Master Home Video Games.*

Becky's relationship with games didn't stop at mastering them. She wanted to *make* them. Six months after she won the *Space Invaders* tournament, she told Arnie Katz, the cofounder of *Electronic Games Magazine*, that she'd taught herself to write code for the Atari 2600 console. Arnie was incredulous. "That's impossible, you're just a kid." Sure, she was, but she was a kid who'd built her own devkit. And won a national tournament. *And* wrote articles on how to be good at games.

Arnie was convinced, so he put Becky in touch with a company in Maryland that desperately needed someone who could program for that console. Within ten minutes of hopping on the phone with the studio, they'd offered her a plane ticket and a job. "And you're 18, right?"

"Yep!" she lied.

And that's how Rebecca started making games professionally when she was still a teenager.

The Original Bard

Over the course of her forty-year career, Rebecca contributed to more than 270 games. She programmed them, wrote them, designed them, created engines, and wrote programming manuals. Basically, she did whatever needed doing. She's made many successful titles, but she's probably best known for *The Bard's Tale III: Thief of Fate.*

After *The Bard's Tale I* and *II*, one of the chief programmers at Interplay, Michael Cranford, left the company. That was fine by Rebecca because it meant she got to throw out his code and start fresh. She hired sci-fi/fantasy writer Michael A. Stackpole to write the story, and she added new playable classes, animation, and audio that the series had never pulled off before. Very few games supported the technical prowess Becky was trying to add to *Bard's Tale III*, but she didn't back down. She even got to include a few beloved *Monty Python and the Holy Grail* references. Oh, and one other thing she introduced to the series? Women characters. It was something she and Cranford had argued over, at length, in the past.

"Where are the girls?" Becky would ask.

And Cranford would answer, "Girls don't play this."

Cranford was obviously wrong (see: this entire book), and his exit meant Rebecca had the freedom to update everything about *Bard's Tale*, from its characters to its engine and programming. Fans loved Becky's new take on the game.

Though *Bard's Tale III* is the game she's known for, her next game, *Dragon Wars*, is the one Becky says she's most proud of. It was supposed to be another *Bard's Tale* game, but a dispute over the name and ownership of the *Bard's Tale* brand forced Becky and the team to rethink it. They changed the setting and name to *Dragon Wars*, a game with very few dragons in it.

Dragon Wars shipped, players and critics loved it, and Interplay continued to grow. Eventually it swelled to five hundred employees. The larger staff was a direct result of Interplay's success, but it was also why Rebecca left the studio in 1995. She wanted to be part of a smaller dev team, so she left to cofound Logicware and, later, Contraband Entertainment, where she worked as an executive. She went on to consult at Electronic Arts, Ubisoft, Bloomberg, Amazon, Microsoft, and Sony.

Burger'll Have Some Sushi

It was in the mid-2000s that Rebecca, already a champion at video games and a legendary creator, truly began to understand herself. In 2003, she came out publicly as transgender. "I kind of knew something was different about me back when I was six or seven, but I just thought it was because my parents kept telling me I was worthless, useless, and kept beating me up all the time," Heineman told *SB Nation* in 2020. "Now, in hindsight, it makes sense. I'm a girl." For her, video games had been an escape from an abusive home and feeling of something *not being quite right*. In 2003, she was able to announce to the world who she really was: a champion, an icon, and Becky.

Becky never retired. Today she runs Olde Sküül, a studio she cofounded with three other women with a ton of games experience: Jennell Jaquays, Maurine Starkey, and Susan Manley. "I'm one of the old-timers who is still in the business," she told *Gamasutra*. "Most old-timers have retired or gone on to greener pastures. What drives me is that I constantly want to learn, better myself as an engineer, better myself as a person. I'm constantly looking for the next best thing."

That passion and motto holds true for more than the games she creates. She served on the board of directors for GLAAD and was the Transgender Chair of Glamazon, Amazon's LGBTQ+ group. She's a pilot, markswoman, mother, and grandmother. She's written award-winning *Sailor Moon* fanfiction. She has a recipe for a cake called "Death by Chocolate," which includes fudge and M&Ms. In short, Becky's great at more than video games.

Now, I know what you've been wondering as you read through this chapter. Does she still keep a bag of burgers in her desk? Do people still call her Burger? The answers are no and sometimes.

While out to dinner with Becky and a few developers from Interplay, Brian Fargo, one of her coworkers, said, "I don't know what's in that tray, but if you eat a big helping of it, I'll pay for your meal." They'd shipped plenty of games by then, and Rebecca had enough money to upgrade above the 29-cent burger, but she wasn't going to turn down a free meal. That's how she was introduced to sushi, now her favorite food.

SIDE QUEST — DORIS SELF

You know those internet jokes about older people and computer literacy? If you tried to make one around Doris Self, she would've laughed at you right before she demolished your high score. In 1984, at fifty-eight years old, she became the world's oldest video game champion on the arcade game Q*bert. *The Guinness Book of World Records* included her in its 2007 printing, though she was eventually unseated by a seventy-two-year-old man. A documentary film, *The King of Kong: A Fistful of Quarters*, followed her quest to beat him and take back her crown.

AMY BRIGGS

Writer of one of the first romance games

P LAYING *PLUNDERED HEARTS*, a text game published by Infocom in 1987, is like waking up inside a romance novel. You're in the captain's quarters of a ship when you hear the clang of swords on the deck above you. The door slams open, and a pirate covered in blood and soot strolls in. *WHAM. SMACK.* You hit him over the head—twice!—with a small chest you found. But another pirate is behind him, one who appears more bemused by your attack than annoyed. You are, in every sense of the word, a damsel in distress. Of course, you don't stay that way. Over the course of your journey, you unravel a kidnapping plot, escape the ship, and cross blades with your enemy. Your unlikely ally, the pirate who attacked your ship, becomes something more: a friend and maybe even your beloved.

Though *Plundered Hearts* might seem familiar to anyone who's read romance novels (like me!), it was a first in many ways for video games. It starred Infocom's first woman protagonist and was the publisher's first romance story. That's thanks to its creator, Amy Briggs. "C. S. Lewis said he had to write the *Chronicles of Narnia* because they were books he wanted to read, and nobody else had written them yet," she said in an interview for Infocom's newsletter, *The Status Line*. "*Plundered Hearts* was a game I wanted to play."

SIDE QUEST

JOYCE KATZ

Polygon, IGN, it's time to meet your granddaddy. If you were a gamer in the early 1980s and needed recs on what to play next, *Electronic Games* was the magazine for you. Joyce Katz was one of its cofounders, and she was among the first video game critics in the United States. *Electronic Games* was also the first of its kind in the US, a magazine devoted entirely to video games. After it eventually shut down, Joyce remained an editor and convention organizer for many years. Without her, gamers would've had a much harder time finding the titles that appealed to them—like an Infocom romance game, or a game called *Zork* that would keep you up all night. Joyce connected gamers to games.

Queen of Hearts (Pre-Plundered Ones)

It was the 1980s, and Amy Briggs was in love with a genre: text adventures. Her boyfriend worked at a computer store and introduced her to 1980's *Ghost Town*, but it was the next game she played, one of Infocom's *Zork* games, that really captured her attention. Before long, she was staying up all night to play. Been there, friend.

At the time, Amy was studying British literature at Macalester College in St. Paul, Minnesota, but when she graduated in 1984, she wasn't sure what to do with her degree or career. She lived with her parents for six months before deciding she wanted to make a clean start and strike out on her own. She moved to Boston without a job or a plan until she came across a wanted ad: Infocom was hiring testers. She applied for the job, wrote an enthusiastic cover letter about how much she loved games, and was hired. The gamer had become the gamedev.

It should have been a dream job, and at first, it probably was. But something had rocked Infocom and the industry at large, which would have a massive effect on Amy and her career: the video game crash of 1983.

Crash and Plunder

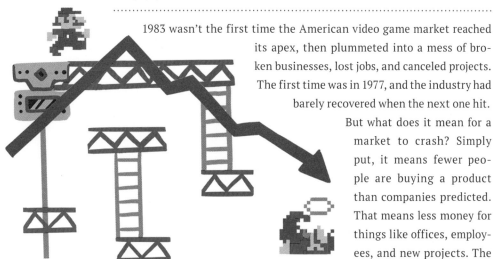

1983 wasn't the first time the American video game market reached its apex, then plummeted into a mess of broken businesses, lost jobs, and canceled projects. The first time was in 1977, and the industry had barely recovered when the next one hit.

But what does it mean for a market to crash? Simply put, it means fewer people are buying a product than companies predicted. That means less money for things like offices, employees, and new projects. The crash, sometimes called "Atari shock," hit the United States the hardest, though it was felt in Japan, too. In 1983, video games made around $3.2 billion, but in 1985, the industry made only $100 million. In two years, the industry's revenues had dropped by 97 percent. Put another way: for every $100 video games earned in 1983, they earned $3 in 1985.

And why, you might be wondering, were people buying fewer games? There are several reasons. The first was that when business leaders saw how much money games were making they pumped in *more* money to make *more* games as fast as they could. Those shorter deadlines meant new games were less polished and, well, less *fun*, so players stopped buying new games.

Another reason boils down to a concept in economics called supply and demand. Here's an example: Say one hundred people are each planning to buy one game console. Five companies realize this, so each company invents a new console and makes one hundred of them, planning to sell all of them. Now there are five hundred consoles available, but still only one hundred people interested in buying one console apiece. That means four hundred consoles go unpurchased. The supply got too big for the demand.

In 1983, there were a ton of new home consoles on the market and a slew of games that had been made quickly and often cheaply, but they weren't selling. Arcade gaming, too, was on the decline. Meanwhile, PC gaming was becoming more popular than ever as computers grew more powerful and smaller. Home computers were growing in popularity, and consoles started to seem superfluous. Hence, the crash—there were too many games and consoles created, and too few people bought them. Console gaming wouldn't begin to recover until the Nintendo Entertainment System, or NES, started gaining popularity in 1985.

When Amy was hired the same year, Infocom hadn't begun its recovery from the crash yet. They'd just released *The Hitchhiker's Guide to the Galaxy*, one of the most beloved text games ever made. Even so, there was a ton of pressure on Infocom's devs not just to make hits, but *ultra-hits*, like *Zork* and *Hitchhiker's*, that would put the company back on the solid footing it had enjoyed before the crash.

Amidst all this, Amy was hired to test games, which meant her days were spent hunting for bugs and trying to fix them. She was promoted to implementor, what we would probably now refer to as a designer, engineer, or programmer. She learned Infocom's coding language and helped translate ideas into games. On the side, she began working on her own project, a game based on her favorite genre of books: romances.

Romance has a lot of subgenres, two of which would inspire Amy's first and only game. One was regency romance, the *Pride and Prejudice*s and *Emma*s of the world. They are often very British and steeped in the societal norms and manners of nineteenth-century England. The other subgenre that inspired her was historical romance, sometimes called "bodice-rippers," lush, passionate novels set in a historical period.

When Amy started writing *Plundered Hearts*, a lot of people she worked with had opinions about it. A designer who'd mentored her urged her to write another game first. That way, she could learn from her mistakes on the first game, then apply those lessons to the one she really cared about. Amy didn't take the advice. Coworkers asked questions, some of which were published and circulated in Infocom's internal newsletter. Among them: "Why a woman as the protagonist?" Until then, Infocom had made gender-neutral, male, or choose-your-gender protagonists, so this was a first. Also, by making her protagonist a woman, Amy invited another question: "Why make that character fall in love?" The subtext being: Was it anti-feminist to star Infocom's first woman protagonist in a kissy game?

"Not really," Amy answered. "Feminism does not rule out romance."

But the questions persisted. "Aren't you really demeaning women, saying that all they're interested in is getting a man? Don't romances portray women as helpless airheads who need Rambo to come help them across the street?"

Amy didn't mince words.

"That's two questions, actually. My answer to the first is that, no, I'm not demeaning women. I don't expect the idea of *Plundered Hearts* to interest all those women who don't like romances, though they would probably enjoy playing it for other reasons. It is not aimed at women, but at romance and adventure lovers, a large number of whom are women.

"As to the second question, you can't get anywhere in *Plundered Hearts* if you act as an air-head. There's your father to be rescued (don't believe that Captain Jamison can do it alone)! There's the hero to be saved from certain death—several times! One doesn't have to be Miss Simper to enjoy dancing (or necking in the gazebo) or be Ms. Rambo to defeat the bad guys. Just be yourself and do both."

Amy was still developing her bodice-romance-literary adventure when Activision bought Infocom. That helped keep the lights on amidst the market crash, but the pressure didn't abate. Infocom still needed bestselling games, or Activision would start laying people off, Amy included.

Into the Unknown (Again)

Plundered Hearts shipped in 1987 to widespread praise from critics, but it didn't sell as well as *Hitchhiker's* or *Zork*. It clocked in at just over 10,000 copies, a respectable number at the time, but not the runaway success Infocom had hoped for.

Still, it's important to remember that sales numbers very rarely reflect a game's quality or its impact on the industry. *Plundered Hearts* came nine years before Lara Croft was invented and twenty years before the *Mass Effect* series embraced romance as part of its core plot. It was released seven years before *Angelique*, the first otome game (more about that on page 30), showed that romantic stories and women leads could carry an entire genre on their shoulders. Reviewers for *Dragon*, *Compute!*, and *ANALOG Computing* all praised the game's prose, challenges, mysteries, and adventure.

Despite that praise, Amy had a difficult time persuading the higher-ups to greenlight her other ideas. She pitched a game based on Anne Rice's *Interview With a Vampire* several years before Rice's books became international bestsellers and were adapted into several movies. Her bosses passed on the pitch—a huge *L* for video games.

Amy left Infocom in 1988, one year before the company went out of business. At her farewell party, her coworkers gave her a sweater emblazoned with the words PULITZER PRIZE WINNER OF 1989. Because whatever Amy wanted to do next, they were confident she'd be the best at it.

They weren't wrong. Amy earned a PhD in cognitive psychology from the University of Minnesota and became a human factors engineer, someone who studies how objects are designed to be used by people. For example, "righty-tighty, lefty-loosey" is a triumph in human factors design.

Though *Plundered Hearts* was Amy's first and only game, it—and Amy herself—were trailblazers. In the 1980s, as video games were shifting from gender-neutral marketing to focusing solely on young boys, Amy understood that many people with many varied interests play, enjoy, and make video games. In just a few years, she went from gamer to gamedev and left her mark on the industry.

YOKO SHIMOMURA

The composer behind your
favorite video game music

THE KÖLNER PHILHARMONIE in Germany is one of the most beautiful concert halls in all of Europe. Its halls have echoed with the cantatas of Bach, the concertos of Mozart, and the symphonies of Beethoven, and in 2019, it was filled with the music of Yoko Shimomura.

It was the eighth stop on the second world tour for the score of *Kingdom Hearts*. The concert had already made appearances in Tokyo, Singapore, Toronto, and New York by the time it reached Cologne, Germany. One of the draws of the concert was a meet-and-greet with Yoko herself, so she'd traveled to the different venues around the world and watched philharmonics perform songs she'd written for the action RPG. Fans eagerly made their way up to her, tears in their eyes as they shook her hand. Seeing their emotion made her own tears well.

Even now, after thirty years in the industry, Yoko is awed and humbled by how much her music means to people. "Like I'm in a dream," she said in a 2019 interview with *OTAQUEST*. "And I'm just trying to stay asleep."

Before the Dream

Yoko was born in 1967 in Hyōgo Prefecture, Japan, and started learning to play the piano when she was still a little girl. She loved classical music and began to create her own compositions, one of which she still remembers (but would never play for anyone because she describes it as "really silly"). By the time she reached junior high, she'd made a promise to herself to see a live orchestra performance at least once per month. No wonder, then, that when it was time to choose a college and area of study, she chose to study piano at the Osaka College of Music.

Then, in 1988, Capcom reached out to Yoko's college looking for a "sound creator" from the class of upcoming graduates. Yoko was about to graduate and had planned to become a piano teacher, but she thought the job sounded interesting. She was excited by the prospect of creating a score like Koji Kondo's *Super Mario Brothers* soundtrack. She asked one of her professors about the job, but she'd studied piano, not composition, so he told her not to bother applying. She ignored him and applied anyway. The application led to an entrance exam, which led to a job offer from Capcom.

Yoko was thrilled to have a job lined up as soon as she graduated, but the people who cared about her weren't as enthused. "My parents cried, my friends were worried, and my teacher was stunned," Yoko said in a 2002 interview with *RocketBaby*. "We're talking about way back when game music wasn't as popular as it is these days."

After her first few days at Capcom, Yoko wasn't sure whether she'd made the right choice, either. Her first few batches of sound effects were rejected, and Yoko wondered whether she belonged in games at all.

A Theme for Every World

Yoko was assigned to the arcade division, where she created 8-bit and 16-bit loops and sound effects for arcade games. "I was a total amateur," Yoko told *Red Bull Music Academy* in 2014, "and relied on courage and bluffing, saying and doing what I could, trying to convince them of my passion for the job." Her dream was to switch from sound effects and 8-bit loops to composing the kind of orchestral, sweeping music she'd grown up with, and she got her first chance on *Street Fighter II*.

> ⇒ 8-bit and 16-bit loops are the kind of music you hear in classic games, like *Space Invaders* and *Mario*. They are electronic, synthesized scores that don't require a ton of memory to play. They're also incredibly catchy.

The *Street Fighter* series began as two-player arcade games. There are eight characters and maps from all over the world to choose from, and Yoko's job was to write original music for each character and each map. Since the maps corresponded to one of the characters, she wanted to capture both the characters' personalities and the maps' cultural and physical settings. It was especially challenging for Yoko because she'd never traveled outside of Japan, and she had no internet to find sounds and scenes from places she'd never been. "My world was still small."

To help broaden her perspective, she turned to *Street Fighter*'s art team. For example, when writing the music for a character named Chun-Li, Yoko looked at the character's design and thought she looked like a modern pop idol. Yoko composed music that captured the same modern, vibrant, poppy energy.

Street Fighter II was released in 1991 and is still considered one of the best fighting games ever made. Part of its success was its music, a score that captured the feeling of traveling the world and meeting colorful, fascinating fighters.

After wondering whether she belonged in games, *Street Fighter II* firmly told Yoko "yes." She loved the work, and now she knew she could do it.

Heart of the Kingdom

After *Street Fighter II*, Yoko worked on the soundtracks and audio design for eleven more Capcom games. But her dream of writing a sweeping, orchestral score for a role-playing game remained; so in 1993, Yoko left Capcom to join Square. While there, Yoko scored more than forty games, but *Kingdom Hearts* holds a special place in her . . . well, her heart.

Not that the project was without its share of pressure. If you aren't familiar with the series, *Kingdom Hearts* takes place in a crossover Square-Enix/Disney universe. Musically speaking, those universes are very, *very* different, and the mashups don't stop there. *Kingdom Hearts* is a blend of genres that have no business working so well together: original characters and licensed ones, Japanese storytelling and Western fairytales, JRPG and action-adventure. Even the setting is confusing to a newcomer: realms of light and darkness, Destiny Islands, Agrabah, Atlantica, the Hundred-Acre Wood, and many more maps and worlds.

Another challenge was the PlayStation 2. It didn't have the memory to play the music of hundred-person philharmonics, so some of Disney's licensed music simply wouldn't work in a video game. Yoko needed to compose around the original scores and adapt already existing tracks to make them work. Specifically, she remembers having to redo music from *The Nightmare Before Christmas* because the length and complexity of the score was impossible to fit into a PS2 game. Yoko experimented, adding new music and discarding some pieces until everything worked. "I'm the type of person that tries until I can't go anymore," she said. "If I can't do it, then I think of another way. I hate to give up, and I have hard time drawing the line."

A fantastic, sprawling, epic score was exactly what Yoko had come to Square to create, but when she was first approached to work on *Kingdom Hearts*, she hesitated. "At first I was like 'Oh, please don't make me do it,'" Yoko told *RocketBaby*. "'I'm sorry, but I can't do it.' I could not imagine what kind of world *Kingdom Hearts* would end up being . . . therefore, I had no idea what type of music I should write!" To figure it out, Yoko read and reread the writers' scripts, pored over concept art, created demo tracks for the director and planners, and sought feedback from the development team. She blended the orchestras of Academy Award–winning Disney composer Alan Menken with her own new, modern music that captured the journey of a new hero, Sora. What resulted was an award-winning, beloved score that toured the most famous concert halls in the world, and the legions of fans who greeted the composer with tears in their eyes.

MANAMI MATSUMAE

SIDE QUEST

DA DA duh DA DA duh duh duh DA DA duh DA DA duh! Recognize it? No? It's the "Game Start" music for *Mega Man*, Capcom's 1987 game that spawned spinoff comics, shows, and additional games. The score was written by Manami Matsumae, who worked with Yoko Shimomura on Capcom's audio team. After leaving Capcom in 1991, she worked as a freelancer and composed for many more games, including *Shovel Knight, SonSon II, Dynasty Wars, U.N. Squadron, Mercs, Magic Sword,* and *Carrier Air Wings*.

Encore

More than thirty years have passed since Yoko joined Capcom and started making loops and sound effects for video games. She's best known for her work on *Kingdom Hearts, Final Fantasy XV, Street Fighter,* and several *Mario* titles, but that's far from all she's done. She's composed music for more than sixty games, arranged music or contributed to the scores of dozens more, and written songs for anime such as *Hi Score Girl* and *Napping Princess*.

And people *adore* her music. They wait in lines to speak with her and cry when they get the chance; they play her music as they walk down the aisle at their weddings or as their final performances in music school. And it all happened because Yoko is "the type of person that tries until I can't go anymore." When her professor told her not to apply to the job at Capcom, she did it anyway. After her sound samples were rejected and she wondered whether she belonged in games, she kept going. When she was handed a project with a massive, sprawling world and limited PS2 hardware, she found a way to make it work. Yoko never gave up on herself, and her work made video game worlds—and the real one—a more musical, vibrant place.

JESSICA CURRY

In *Dear Esther*, the narrator tells a story of love and loss as the player explores quiet caves and wildflower-covered hillsides. "The Narrator's language is dense and poetic," Jessica Curry said in a 2017 *Gamasutra* interview, "contradictory and powerful, and there is an emotional pulse that runs through the writing that just made my soul sing." The writing inspired Jessica to compose *Dear Esther*'s score. Jessica and her husband worked on the game together and became cofounders of a studio called The Chinese Room. In 2013, the audio design for *Dear Esther* was nominated for a BAFTA award, one of the most prestigious in the business. Three years later, her score for *Everybody's Gone to the Rapture,* which she considers her first truly interactive piece of music, won both the Best Music and Best Audio BAFTA awards.

JADE RAYMOND

The builder behind a thousand creators

I T'S HARD TO describe the chaotic, bubbly energy of E3, the annual trade show held in the heart of Los Angeles every year. It's not open to the public, and the game developers, publishers, retailers, and journalists who make up its attendees need a special pass to attend. The exposition swallows several downtown blocks, with walls and windows across downtown plastered with billboards for upcoming games. Gamedevs with plastic badges swinging from lanyards camp out at every restaurant and microbrewery within a three-mile radius.

Now imagine all that, but in 2006. The top songs on the radio are "Bad Day" and "Hips Don't Lie," George W. Bush is still president of the United States, and the most popular show on TV is *CSI: Crime Scene Investigation*. The E3 audience has swelled to more than 60,000 people, and they're all waiting, wondering: What's coming next? What's everyone making? What will be the next big thing in games? Enter: Jade Raymond.

She takes the stage alongside another Ubisoft developer. She narrates while he plays Ubisoft's up-and-coming game. This is the first time anyone's seen it on the Xbox 360, and she explains the technical ins and outs of the gameplay and the engine. The game they're showing off? It's a new franchise called *Assassin's Creed*.

Yes, *that Assassin's Creed*.

"Why Not Me?"

Jade was born in 1975 and grew up in Montréal, Québec, and she started playing games when she was around six years old. Her cousins had that most exclusive of 1980s toys, a computer, so she went to their house to play text adventures. When her family finally bought an Atari console, she dove into games like *Pong* and *Space Invaders*.

Around the same time, Jade's family bought an Apple II computer, and she discovered LEGO Mindstorms, which was a kit you could use to build a robot. Just as cool, you could learn basic programming on your computer and use it to *control* the robot. Through Mindstorms, she discovered a love for building hardware and software.

Jade was around sixteen years old when the thought occurred to her: someone had to be making the games she loved. "Why not me?" She decided to study computer science and minor in art history at McGill University, also in Québec. She completed several internships before she landed her first job as a programmer with Sony Online, and within a couple of years, she was promoted to a management position. Then she took a job with Electronic Arts, this time as a producer instead of a programmer.

It's difficult to describe the workload of a video game producer because every studio and publisher treats them a little differently. In short, producers make sure games get made. They negotiate between developers and publishers, organize schedules, help set goals for departments, manage money, communicate changes across teams, and help with staffing. Without producers, the game development process would quickly become a disorganized, soul-draining, expensive mess—and many games would never make it out of production.

After Jade produced *The Sims Online* for EA, she worked for a start-up before joining Ubisoft, one of the biggest publishers in the world. When she joined, Ubisoft asked her what she wanted to work on rather than assigning her to a project already in development. Jade's answer was a simple one: she wanted to make a game that she'd want to play. That meant something "pulse-pounding," something with action and adventure. Ubisoft sent Jade around the world to visit their studios and see if any of the projects appealed to her. She traveled to Vancouver, Los Angeles, and London before finally landing in Montréal, where she found the project she was looking for.

The team at Ubisoft Montréal had recently shipped *Prince of Persia: Sands of Time* to fan and critical acclaim. They wanted to make another action-heavy, high-stakes, epic adventure game, but one that felt different from *Prince of Persia*. The plan was to make a game based loosely on the real-life Order of Assassins and its founder, Hassan-i Sabbah. After talking to the team and seeing their work, Jade knew she wanted to help. It was time for her to move back to Montréal.

SIOBHAN REDDY

SIDE QUEST

For many years, Siobhan Reddy avoided cameras, journalists, and social media, leading *Kotaku* to dub her "the invisible woman" in 2014. At the time, she was the director of the studio Media Molecule, and she preferred being in the office to being out on the press junket. Then, while serving on a BAFTA committee, Siobhan read surveys that showed very few girls believed they could grow up to be game developers. That's why Siobhan decided to start talking to the media: to give little girls someone to look up to. Born in 1979 in South Africa and raised in Australia, Siobhan grew up playing games with her brother. She started at Media Molecule as an executive producer before becoming the studio director, and she's won many awards for production and innovation, including a 2021 BAFTA Fellowship for "her pioneering work on advocacy for diversity, inclusion, and creative and collaborative working culture."

Living by the Creed

When Jade joined the *Assassin's Creed* team, they weren't just building the game; they were also building the Scimitar engine that would power it. The engine was designed to make climbing, the defining mechanic of the *Assassin's Creed* series, more fluid and natural-looking, in addition to other improvements. And, to add even more pressure, the Scimitar engine wouldn't just be used for *Assassin's Creed*, but for Ubisoft's PlayStation 3 and Xbox 360 games *going forward*.

Jade loved it. The high-stress, high-yield environment was exactly the kind she thrived in. "I'm a person who loves change and loves putting myself in crazy, difficult situations," Jade told *Polygon* in 2015. "It's funny, because every year you go to these events like DICE or wherever, and everybody's talking about, 'Oh my God, disruption in the game industry, and it's crazy.' But it's like, 'Haven't you been in the game industry forever, and hasn't there been this crazy disruption every single year?' Either it's social games on Facebook, oh no, now it's mobile, oh no, now it's Early Access, now it's VR and HoloLens."

When it came time to show off *Assassin's Creed* in demos, trailers, and interviews, Jade was often the one behind the microphone or on the stage. She praised the technical and creative achievements of her team, and when *Assassin's Creed* shipped, critics and players agreed. Today, the franchise includes games, comics, graphic novels, books, and films.

Yet the debut of the franchise introduced something new and ugly into Jade's career: harassment. In 2007, the same year *Assassin's Creed* shipped, a website hosted a horribly sexist, inappropriate comic of Jade. Ubisoft issued a take-down notice, and the website complied. It was awful, but Jade said in a 2007 *GameReactor* interview that what really irritated her was when people casually dismissed her ten years of experience to focus on her looks.

It's difficult to find a conversation with Jade in which the interviewer doesn't ask her how she feels about being a woman in games, or whether she finds it difficult to be attractive in this job. Yes, really, and if you're rolling your eyes, that's a totally valid response. Jade mostly laughs off these inquiries or gives answers like: "I'm a producer, and I do my job. . . . When I get interviewed by the media, I do get a lot of questions about being a girl. . . . I kind of wish that it wasn't so different. It's kind of like being a Canadian and working on a game, or being part Chinese and working on a game. . . . I'm a woman, and it gets a lot of attention for no reason, in my opinion."

In 2017, a *Mic* article called Jade "the first casualty" of a harassment culture that included, but was not limited to, Gamergate. The article is well-researched, but calling Jade a "casualty" isn't correct. Being a casualty implies that the harassment she faced destroyed her or her career. It didn't. Jade remains one of the most prolific game developers of our time—and she isn't even close to done.

Creating a Haven

Like any developer who's been in games for a while, Jade's had both wins and losses. She helped found Motive Studios and Ubisoft Toronto. She also worked on a *Star Wars* game with

Amy Hennig (she's on page 52) that was canceled, and she was a vice president at Google who oversaw Google Stadia, a cloud gaming service.

"Several people have asked me recently: 'After all of these experiences, do you still want to be in the games industry?'" Jade wrote on the PlayStation blog in March 2021. "The answer is always an unwavering YES! The games industry is where I belong!

"Whether it's playing *Settlers of Catan* with my kids or *Valheim* with my team, games continue to bring me joy. They're a way to relax, connect, and share experiences with people I care about. And the act of making games is, in many ways, even more fulfilling."

The blogpost announced Jade's next project: Haven, a studio in Montréal backed by Sony, that Jade would build from the ground up. As she did with Motive and Ubisoft Toronto, her job was to build a team and project, brick by brick.

It's easy to imagine a younger Jade patiently putting the blocks of LEGO Mindstorms together, then hopping on her Apple II computer to make her robot move exactly as designed. It's what she does in games, too: assembles the teams, gives them the direction they need to make something amazing, then watches them go.

KARIN WEEKES

During Karin Weekes's job interview with BioWare, the devs asked her: What would you do with a holodeck? In *Star Trek*, the holodeck creates an immersive virtual reality that can create any place, and any person, you could possibly imagine. Karin paused and considered the question. Then she told them her answer was a little too risqué to say out loud. Boom, she was hired.

BioWare needed someone who could speak openly, thoughtfully, and honestly about sex and romance, and if you've played their games, it's not hard to see why. BioWare has become famous for the romances in its games, including Liara and Garrus (*Mass Effect*); Alistair, Dorian, and Morrigan (*Dragon Age*); Bastila and Aric (*Knights of the Old Republic*); and many more beautiful, loveable folks. Karin's holodeck answer landed her a job as BioWare's first editor. She's now one of a team of editors who comb through thousands of lines of text and dialogue, checking for lore discrepancies as well as grammar and "character voice" (i.e., making sure a character written by different writers doesn't sound wildly different from scene to scene). It's a big job, and Karin was the first at BioWare to show how necessary editors are to make big, beautiful, beloved, story-driven games.

JOYCE WEISBECKER

The first woman to program
a video game, period

I T WAS THE summer of 1976, and a home console, the RCA Studio II, was about to launch. It lacked just one important feature, and that was . . . games. Since those are pretty important for a console launch, the engineer behind the Studio II turned to one of his testers for help: his eighteen-year-old daughter.

And, honestly? She wasn't all that interested.

She was killing time the summer before she started college at Rider University. However, her father insisted: she didn't have anything better to do, and the coding experience would look good on her résumé. She agreed, and that's how, at eighteen years old, Joyce Weisbecker became one of the first women game designers, programmers, and indie developers in the business.

A Family of Many Hobbies

The way Joyce's parents met sounds like something out of a rom-com. Her father, Joseph, met her mother in 1955, and he charmed her by talking about the future: things like tiny computers that could fit into things like typewriters and refrigerators, a ludicrous proposition at a time when most computers took up entire rooms. Given his interests and those of Joyce's mother, a teacher, it's no wonder that Joyce grew up playing and loving video games.

Joyce was born in 1958 in New Jersey, and from the time she was small, she loved visiting RCA, the electronics company where her father worked as an engineer. In the mid-1960s, engineers there were working on a prototype billiards video game, and Joyce was one of its earliest—and youngest—players.

Outside of the office, Joseph had another prototype in the works. He wanted to build a computer at home, but the kits to make them were scarce and expensive. At the time, computers that could fit comfortably on a desk were called "minicomputers" and could cost anywhere from $6,000 to $25,000. At the time, the average American salary was around $11,000 per year. Undeterred, Joseph bought parts from different electronics stores and assembled his computer from nothing. Though building a computer from parts isn't an uncommon hobby today, it simply wasn't done in the 1960s. But Joseph did it, and Joyce played with the computer he was building. Joseph's project would eventually evolve into a computer called FRED: Flexible Recreational & Educational Device.

Though FRED began its life as a computer, it would soon become something even newer to the technology scene: a game console.

From FRED To Console

After Joyce's father built FRED in his basement, he set it up on the enclosed back porch of their home. Naturally, Joyce and her sister wanted to play with it. It would have been easy to tell them no, that they were too young and the technology was too delicate, but Joseph didn't. When Joyce started tinkering with the code that ran FRED, he encouraged her to keep going and keep learning.

But while FRED was experiencing a successful home launch among the Weisbeckers, RCA's future was a little dimmer. Joseph's bosses at RCA thought his ideas about tiny computers in appliances and game consoles were far-fetched. At the same time, RCA had lost millions of dollars that they'd invested in massive mainframe computers—a loss that would be hard to swallow even today and must have seemed impossible to overcome back then.

Even so, in 1973, RCA decided to take a chance on two of Joseph's ideas. The first was FRED: RCA began building minicomputers based on Joseph's design. The second took a little more convincing. Joseph was certain that home consoles were the next big thing in video games, and he thought RCA should build one. Some of his coworkers were skeptical. After all, video games might just be a fad, a bright and shiny pastime that faded as quickly as it had begun. Joseph convinced them it was worth exploring, and RCA began production on its first console, the RCA Studio II. (There is no published Studio I, and I can't tell you why. Let's assume it was for a good reason.)

RCA was building game hardware, but they didn't see a reason to hire a game designer or programmer. Instead, the company decided to hire a teenager who'd grown up playing with FRED's code and knew it almost as well as its creator. Joyce was hired, on contract, to create games for the Studio II. Today, she calls herself the first indie game developer.

Schoolhouse Gawk

During the summer between her senior year of high school and her freshman year of college, Joyce created her first game for the RCA Studio II, *TV Schoolhouse I*. It took Joyce a week to code. To create the game, Joyce used pen and paper to write out assembly code, then entered it into a FRED prototype using a keypad. The FRED prototype was similar enough to the Studio II that it could feed information to the console, and—voilà—Joyce had created a game.

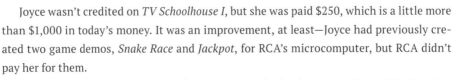

Joyce wasn't credited on *TV Schoolhouse I*, but she was paid $250, which is a little more than $1,000 in today's money. It was an improvement, at least—Joyce had previously created two game demos, *Snake Race* and *Jackpot*, for RCA's microcomputer, but RCA didn't pay her for them.

Like many early games, *TV Schoolhouse I* came with a book meant to be used during play. For some games, this was an instruction manual or level map. For *TV Schoolhouse I*, it was a book of questions. To play the game, one player read a question from the book, and the other typed in a multiple-choice answer on the Studio II's keypad. The game kept track of right and wrong answers, tallying up the score at the end to name a winner.

Two months after shipping *TV Schoolhouse I*, RCA needed more games for the Studio II, so they turned to their most prolific—and, well, only—designer. She created two. *Speedway* was a two-player racing game with little white rectangles that sped across the screen. In *Tag*, another two-player game, each player controlled a dot and tried not to get tagged by the other dot. One player's dot was "It," and the goal was to not be tagged for two minutes.

Both games were simple, but that didn't make them any less challenging to create. "People who work with modern computers don't understand the restrictions," Joyce told *Fast Company* in 2017. "You had the equivalent of two black-and-white 32-by-32 Windows icons, and that was your entire screen."

In the next two years, Joyce made eight more games for RCA, all while working within the confines of the Studio II and early televisions. For any game designer, eight games in two years is an impressive pace. For a fresh-out-of-high-school, self-taught programmer, it's incredible. Unfortunately, Joyce being incredible wasn't enough to save the Studio II. In a year, the Studio II sold between 53,000 and 64,000 units, not enough to be profitable. The biggest reason for this was that the Atari 2600, a more powerful console with more games, launched the same year as RCA's first console. In 1978, RCA announced they would stop making the Studio II.

Though the console was history, Joyce was only getting started. In 1977, she made three more video games for the COSMAC VIP minicomputer. *Slide*, *Sum Fun*, and *Sequence Shoot* were Joyce's last projects for RCA, all completed while she was in college. They were the last games she would create . . . at least, for the next forty-some years.

Choose Your Own Future

In the 1970s, video games were a hobby for a niche audience: those who could afford and were interested in owning and operating non-user-friendly computers. Which meant coders, mainly. Even Roberta Williams (page 1) marketed most of her early games to programmers and computer scientists. Video games had a small audience that would eventually grow large enough to fuel Roberta's career and Sierra On-Line, but Joyce wasn't part of this technical revolution.

After her first year of college, Joyce decided to study computer engineering and actuarial science. She worked as an actuary, a person whose job is to predict and minimize financial risk, before returning to school and eventually becoming an engineer.

Though she has been many things since her first job as a programmer, Joyce hasn't given up on games for good. She told *Fast Company*, "I'm trying to gear up to do really interesting AI and computer-assisted animation. Because I realize I want to do story-based cooperative games." A story-based co-op game designed by the first female video game programmer? Yeah, I want to play it, and you should, too.

LAURA NIKOLICH

Designer and programmer of the first web-slinger video game

T HE YEAR IS 2016, and we are once again at E3. An announcement trailer is about to debut from Insomniac Games. The screen goes dark, and a voice says, "People see me and think they're safer. But it's not really me they're seeing." The New York skyline shifts into view, and Spider-Man appears, clinging to a wall and looking very cool doing it. *Marvel's Spider-Man*, released in 2018, is one of the most well-regarded superhero games ever made, but it wasn't Peter Parker's first appearance in a video game. That would be *Spider-Man* on the Atari 2600, and its creator was Laura Nikolich, the first person to write, design, and program the iconic web-slinger.

Spider-Man, Spider-Man, does whatever an Atari 2600 can.

Which, in 1982, wasn't a lot, so Laura had her work cut out for her.

A Chance Meeting

Rewind thirty-five years, from 2016 back to 1981. Laura wanders a hotel lobby, waiting for her client to arrive. She works in Boston at a company that creates financial software—and she hates her job. She hates the office politics, the cutthroat attitude, and the work itself.

While she's killing time, she wanders around until she stumbles into a job fair hosted by Parker Brothers. She's heard of them, of course: Parker Brothers is the publisher behind board games like *Monopoly* and *Clue*. Laura walks in and strikes up a conversation with the Parker Brothers employees, and they assume she's lost. She's wearing formal business attire, and if you've ever been to E3 or GDC, you know that most of us only ever wear game-branded T-shirts, sneakers, jeans, and sometimes a blazer (if we're feeling fancy). Formalwear or no, Laura ends up speaking with Jim McGinnis, the hiring manager, and she tells him about the work she did in real-time programming at Motorola. Unbeknownst to Laura, Parker Brothers has just decided to try making video games, which makes Laura's experience very relevant. Jim invites her to interview with the company. She does, and Parker Brothers hires her *on the spot*. Just like that, Laura is Parker Brothers' fifth game programmer. Ever.

But what was the job, exactly? Laura had studied engineering and business, and she'd coded before, but she had no experience writing, designing, or programming a video game. What had she gotten herself into?

Swinging Past Limitations

The job was, as it turned out, to create the first Spider-Man video game. When Laura started as a game designer at Parker Brothers in the fall of 1981, the deal with Marvel was already in place. She arrived at Parker Brothers, settled in at her desk, and started working on the first video game based on a Marvel comic.

One of the common misconceptions about game development is that the hardest part is coming up with ideas, when really, the hardest part is trying to fit your ideas into what current-generation machines can handle. That means considering how much memory you have to work with (Yoko Shimomura dealt with this a *lot* on arcade games, page 88). It's a constraint that gamedevs deal with in the era of the Xbox Series X and PlayStation 5, and it was even more challenging in the early days of Atari consoles. In Laura's case, the console in question was the Atari 2600. Though it was a technical marvel (*ha!*) for its time—a small arcade box that could be hooked into a home TV set—its games had to be simple, or the console couldn't run them. That meant limited colors, sounds, shapes, and animations. Laura was under these constraints while simultaneously trying to capture the look and feel of the most popular character in Marvel Comics history.

Even so, Laura was having a *blast* at her new job. She describes her time at Parker Brothers as the best in her career, a creative and collaborative day-to-day that she adored. With a collaborative environment to support her, Laura got to work on a prototype.

The first challenge was Spider-Man's suit: an iconic red and blue, but very hard to pull off with the Atari 2600's limited color palette. Laura tweaked it, making subtle but important changes to the code until his suit was recognizable to any Spidey fan. Next, the gameplay. Laura decided the game would be a vertical scroller as Spider-Man swung up a skyscraper. She chose the Green Goblin as the game's main enemy for two reasons. One, he's a major Spider-Man villain. Two, he could fly, which meant Laura could program him to float around the screen and threaten the player. In addition to the Green Goblin, Laura scattered bandits around the skyscraper and had them plant bombs that the player needed to disable.

Six months after Laura started at Parker Brothers, the game was ready to ship. She'd pushed the limits of what the Atari 2600 console could do, but would it be enough? Would anyone want to play *Spider-Man*?

The answer was yes, and it was helped along by a robust marketing campaign that showed how much Parker Brothers believed in Laura's creation. In 1982, *Spider-Man* got its own TV commercial, in which the titular character plays the game while the Green Goblin mocks him (ugh, rude). In the March 1983 issue of *Blip: The Video Game Magazine*, Spider-Man made the cover. The headline was "Spider-Man Plays SPIDER-MAN," and the interior photos don't disappoint. Spider-Man and Green Goblin (or guys in those costumes, but who can say?) play the game against each other while

Stan Lee and a group of kids look on. Yes, *the* Stan Lee—though he admitted the kids got a better score.

Spiders, Goblins, and Care Bears, Oh My

Like most game designers, Laura didn't take much of a break after *Spider-Man* shipped in 1982. Instead, she began work on a *Care Bears* game, which likely would've shipped the same year or in 1983.

Laura considers *Care Bears* her greatest achievement because the technical limitations she faced and overcame were even greater than the ones in *Spider-Man*. Unfortunately, *Care Bears* was very nearly completed—in its final stages of playtesting, in fact—when Parker Brothers decided not to ship it. The reason had nothing to do with Laura's design or work and everything to do with how Parker Brothers planned, or didn't plan, to market it. According to Laura, Parker Brothers had already decided to target teenage boys as its primary video game audience (*sigh*, see Brenda Laurel's chapter on page 37). Since *Care Bears* appeals to little kids, they didn't think they could sell it.

Laura didn't agree with the decision, but she was a professional, so she got to work on her next project, *Frogger II: ThreeeDeep!* It was the sequel to the original 1981 *Frogger* game, and this time, she didn't create it alone. Two other programmers handled code for the Atari 8-bit series, the Atari 5200, and the Atari 2600, and Laura programmed the game for the ColecoVision console. When it shipped in 1984, gaming critics called it flawless and challenging, a perfect sequel to the first beloved game.

Unfortunately, the good times wouldn't last.

A Strong Case of PBBS

E.T. The Extraterrestrial is half video game, half urban legend. The legend goes that *E.T.* is the worst video game ever made and nearly singlehandedly crashed the gaming industry. Atari was so ashamed of it, they buried twelve million copies in the Alamogordo desert of New Mexico and covered it with cement.

It's a wacky, wild, fun story . . . and a bit of an overstatement, both in regard to *E.T.*'s quality and the whole crashing-the-industry thing. *E.T.* was one of the games swept up in the video game crash of 1983, which I talked about at length in Amy Briggs's chapter on page 83. I mentioned there that it's sometimes referred to as "Atari shock," and the reason is this: Before the crash, Atari poured a lot of money into *E.T.* and a port of *Pac-Man*. A port means a game originally designed for one console is remade for another. In this case, *Pac-Man* was an arcade game that was remade for the Atari 2600. Both games were rushed, and gamers disliked them so much that people started to lose faith that Atari games, and home consoles in general, were worth buying. The Nintendo Entertainment System would eventually help revive the home console business in North America and Japan, but not in time to save Laura's job. She was laid off in 1984, along with hundreds of game designers at Parker Brothers and across America.

It was an awful situation but not a total surprise. Many designers knew Atari was in trouble, and Laura said the "heart" had gone out of their creative projects. "Nothing lasts forever," she said. "I'm just glad I was a part of it." After Parker Brothers announced the layoffs, one of her coworkers hosted a party and had custom buttons made. The buttons were emblazoned with the words, "ANOTHER SAD CASE OF PBSS," which stood for "Parker Brothers Spoiled Syndrome." "And he was right," Laura said. "No other job measured up to that great experience. I still have my button."

AYA KYOGOKU

Animal Crossing: New Horizons saved the world. Okay, not really, but in 2020, it connected a ton of people who desperately needed it. The game shipped the same year COVID-19 sent the world into quarantine, and it was the soothing multiplayer experience people needed. Aya Kyogoku, the game's director, has an extensive background working on Nintendo titles. Before working on the *Animal Crossing* series, she was a writer on *The Legend of Zelda: Twilight Princess* and several other games in the *Animal Crossing* and *Legend of Zelda* canon.

After working on *Animal Crossing: New Leaf*, which appealed to more women than Nintendo had ever been able to reach before, Aya told *Wired* magazine, "Having worked on this team where there were almost equal numbers of men and women made me realize that [diversity] can open you up to hearing a greater variety of ideas and sharing a greater diversity of ideas." She argues that gender diversity on teams creates better, more broadly appealing games. Considering *Animal Crossing: New Horizons* is the second-bestselling game created for the Nintendo Switch—second only to *Mario Kart Deluxe*—it looks like she's right.

My Mom Made That

Though she doesn't work in games anymore, they have remained a big part of Laura's life. In fact, two of her four sons went on to become game developers. One day at work, one of Laura's sons casually told his friends that his mom made the first *Spider-Man* game, but they didn't believe him. Naturally, he whipped out his phone, pulled up a few articles, and showed off her work. "No way," was the friend's response. "Did your mom really do that? YOUR MOM?!"

Yes, his mom. Laura Nikolich, creator of the first video game Spider-Man, someone with a bad, bad case of PBSS and an early icon of the industry.

BRENDA ROMERO

The mechanic behind the message

I N BRENDA ROMERO'S best-known game, *Train*, nobody wins. Upon reaching the end, players have been nauseated, flushed, and heartsick. Some even wept. Of the dozens who have played, only one person has ever wanted to play it again. Just as Brenda designed it.

Train is one in a series of board games Brenda created called *The Mechanic is the Message*. The purpose of the series isn't to have fun, make money, or launch a franchise, but to explore, through play, what it means to be human. "A game is all I know," Brenda told the *Wall Street Journal* in 2009. "I don't work in another medium."

For more than forty years, video and board games have been Brenda's means of communication and artistic expression—which, by the way, makes her the most veteran woman game developer out there. During her career, she's challenged and shaped how game design is taught, practiced, and expressed, and for that work, she's won a Lifetime Achievement Award, a Fulbright Fellowship, as well as awards from BAFTA and the Game Developers Conference.

Not bad for someone who broke into the games industry at fifteen years old.

Wait, She Was Fifteen?

Yes, you read that right. When Brenda was fifteen years old, she got a job at Sir-Tech Software manning the tip line. This was 1981, so players didn't have Google or *Polygon* walkthroughs if they needed help with a puzzle or a boss fight. Instead, they had a tip line they could call for help, and Brenda was on the other end. Even before Brenda joined Sir-Tech, she says she can't remember a time when she wasn't playing or creating games. She loved to build houses out of LEGOs and invite people to walk through them. No wonder that she eventually became a level designer.

But how did a fifteen-year-old get that job? By talking with another teenage gamedev, obviously. Linda Currie (you can read more about her on page 122) cofounded Sir-Tech with her brothers. One day, Linda was in the girls' bathroom asking around for a non-menthol cigarette. Brenda shared one, and the two struck up a conversation. Linda asked Brenda if she had a job. Nope. Had Brenda heard of Sir-Tech? Nope. *Wizardry*? Nada. *Dungeons & Dragons*? Yes! More than twenty years and many, many game awards later, Brenda said, "I got lucky. If I had answered that question wrong—'Have you got a job?' 'Yup,'—my whole future would have changed."

Brenda continued to work for Sir-Tech through high school and college. She considered working in software or computer technology, interviewing at places like IBM, after she graduated from Clarkson University in Ogdensburg, New York. But when she realized what her day-to-day would look like, she decided to stick with games. Her colleagues at Sir-Tech knew Brenda had been interviewing for other jobs, so when she told them she'd decided to stick around and make games with them instead, they were thrilled.

"Nowadays parents think it's odd when kids say they want to grow up and be a game designer," Brenda said in a 2007 interview with MTV. "Imagine it's 1989 when I was saying it, right? I might as well have just said, 'I want to be Marlon Brando,' or 'I want to be a rock star.'" (Marlon Brando was a mega-famous actor in the twentieth century, in case you were wondering.)

Brenda calls the next few years of her career "almost like an apprenticeship." She worked with some of the industry's earliest and best designers, receiving a hands-on education that most gamedevs could only dream of. When the designers who were mentoring her had too much work, she picked up the slack, and she began to design her own games, too. "I loved it," she said. "It was really working with digital LEGOs."

During her eighteen years at Sir-Tech, Brenda worked in several roles, including tester, designer, and writer. She was a writer on the *Jagged Alliance* series and designer-slash-writer on *Wizardry 8*, which was named RPG of the Year in 2001 by *Computer Gaming World*.

Then, in a twist far too common for gamedevs (including yours truly), it all came crashing down around her. Sir-Tech closed its doors the same year *Wizardry 8* was released to critical and fan acclaim. Sir-Tech was unable to compete with larger studios and publishers, and after nearly twenty years at the company, Brenda needed to start interviewing again. This time, with the goal to stay in game development.

LESLIE SCOTT

Build a tower out of blocks, then take the blocks out one by one. Take the wrong one out, and down the tower goes. The popular party game *Jenga* was a staple in Western households throughout the 1980s and '90s, and, like Brenda Romero's board games, *Jenga* combines simple design with brilliant challenge. The game requires very few rules to get started, making it a perfect game for kids—or adults who don't feel like reading a rulebook. Oh, and did we mention its creator? Leslie Scott designed the iconic game, which debuted at the 1983 London Toy Fair. Eight years later, she founded the board game company Oxford Games Ltd.

The New Radical

Thankfully, Brenda didn't stay unemployed long. After Sir-Tech folded, she joined Atari to work on *Dungeons & Dragons: Heroes* for Xbox, which released in 2003. She then worked for Cyberlore Studios, where she made a game that cemented her reputation as one of the "new radicals," *Nerve* magazine's 2006 list of "the 50 artists, actors, authors, activists and icons who are making the world a more stimulating place." That game was 2005's *Playboy: The Mansion*.

In the game, you play as Hugh Hefner, the founder of *Playboy Magazine*, and your goal is to build the Playboy brand up from nothing. As you do, you can design the interior of the Playboy Mansion and host parties there. You might think designing and publishing a magazine, building an empire, and partying in your mansion would be enough to fill your time, but no, you can also build different kinds of relationships with the NPCs—casual, business, or romantic.

It's important to remember the era in which Brenda was designing this game. For decades, video games have had a hot-cold relationship with portrayals of sex. Even in genres like otome (read more about it on page 30), *how much* games should portray, and how seriously those games should be taken as works of art, is often in question. For example, you might remember the "Hot Coffee" scandal of the mid-2000s, and if not, that's why you're reading this book. In 2005, a fan-made mod for the game *Grand Theft Auto: San Andreas*, which had come out the year before, revealed old, unused code that players could use to create a minigame that ended in a player-controlled sex scene. This was a *huge* deal: it led to a class-action lawsuit, which Rockstar Games, creator of *Grand Theft Auto*, settled in 2008, promising $35 to anyone offended by the scene. Lawmakers, including then-US Senator Hillary Clinton, called for stricter regulations on video game sales and ratings.

It was amidst this controversy that Brenda was designing a game *intentionally* about sex, so it's no wonder that Brenda became a passionate anti-censorship advocate. The same year as the "Hot Coffee" scandal, Brenda founded the International Game Developers Sex Special Interest Group (Sex SIG), which described its purpose as: "[Sex SIG] embraces sex and sexuality as a natural, healthy, and positive force in our lives and in the games we make." The SIG still exists under the umbrella of the International Game Developers Association, now covering romance as well as sex. In 2013, Brenda published a book on the subject, *Sex in Video Games*.

To sum Brenda's career up simply, she'd become a "new radical" in every sense of the word—and she certainly made games, and pop culture, more interesting.

The Game Artiste

In 2010, Roger Ebert famously said, "Video games can never be art." But Roger Ebert never met Brenda Romero.

Brenda is credited on fifty games (both board and video) and counting, but none hits quite as hard or in the same way as *Train*, the game that made people weep. On its surface, the board game is simple: There are several sets of train tracks, and players are each assigned boxcars. The players attempt to fill those boxcars with as many tiny yellow figurines as they can and move their boxcar along the track to a finish line. Players draw cards that either help them move their boxcars forward or force them to abandon some of their figurines. When a train does cross the finish line, the destination is revealed to be a concentration camp. The game is a representation of the Holocaust.

For Brenda, *Train* was a personal, heart-wrenching act of creation. She wanted to explore the role of complicity in the Holocaust and how people could blindly follow orders

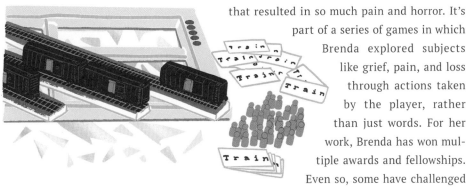

that resulted in so much pain and horror. It's part of a series of games in which Brenda explored subjects like grief, pain, and loss through actions taken by the player, rather than just words. For her work, Brenda has won multiple awards and fellowships. Even so, some have challenged Brenda's decision to turn the Holocaust into a game, wondering if by doing so she has trivialized one of the most horrific events in history. "I don't see it as something that trivializes," Brenda told *The Wall Street Journal* in 2009. "Rather, I see it as the medium finally reaching a new potential."

And this was the point of her work: that because games are an active medium, unlike movies or books, they have the power to explore emotions and actions rather than simply *showing* the audience an event separate from themselves. If a movie can make you feel empathy and understand what happened during a horrific event, games can help you understand *why* people took the actions they did—because you, by virtue of playing the game, are taking action, too.

Today, Brenda and her husband are co-owners of Romero Games, where they create whatever idea sparks their imagination: from 2020's *Empire of Sin*, a video game about running a mob, to 2017's *Gunman Taco Truck*, a roguelike pitched by Brenda's then-twelve-year-old son. It's been more than forty years since Brenda chatted with her friend in a girls' bathroom and landed a job at a fledgling game studio. Since then, she has devoted almost her entire life—and, if you count the period with the LEGOs, then her whole life—to exploring and expanding the medium of games.

Games have become a second language to her, and through her work, we're all able to explore the actions and emotions that make us human.

MARY FLANAGAN

The book *Critical Play: Radical Game Design* changed the way people saw games, and it changed the way game designers saw themselves. Mary Flanagan's book examined the ways artists and activists have used games throughout history to critique social structures. One of her standout works is *[Grace:AI]*, an artificial intelligence *designed* to be feminist: it learns about life, art, and history *only* through the lens of women artists throughout history. "The artists I have chosen as her 'teachers' are outspoken, strong individuals who worked or work in the male-dominated art world." Mary's book and games cross the borders of game design, art, and critical theory, uniting them all to remind everyone that video games *can* be high art.

MEGAN GAISER

The CEO of "un-Barbie"

S TOP ME IF you've heard this one: women don't play video games. If you haven't, you must run in pretty awesome circles. If you have, it's probably because you exist on the internet. Though it's less of a talking point and more of a fringe opinion in the 2020s, in the 1990s and early 2000s, critics and gamers (and, later, people with way too many numbers in their Twitter handles) liked to argue that women don't play games and are "computer-phobic" in general. Unfortunately, that opinion wasn't limited to people outside the games industry, and it was people like Megan and those in the Purple Games Movement (see page 38) who fought against it.

Computer-phobic? Uninterested in games? Megan didn't buy it, so she helped craft a series of games designed with little girls in mind—and turned a studio into a multimillion-dollar business.

Glued to the Screen

By the time Megan joined the games industry in the 2000s, women had been making video games for more than twenty years. Forty, if we want to get technical and include Mabel Addis Mergardt, and, *yes, we do*! Despite this, very few publishers and studios were led by women. Roberta Williams was one of the exceptions, and she retired the year Megan was named CEO of Her Interactive.

Oops, spoilers. Okay, backing up a bit.

From the time she was small, Megan loved films and wanted to tell stories that touched people's hearts. She studied English at Towson University, and after she graduated in 1981, she moved to Washington, DC, and worked for a father-son team who taught her how to make films. For the next eleven years, she was a producer and editor co-creating educational, corporate, and documentary films and videos.

Her career was going well, but she was curious about games and other multimedia projects that were springing up along the West Coast. In particular, she wanted to tell stories about women, and she wondered how interactive media would expand on the linear, passive stories found in films. Megan's sister lived in Seattle, Washington, so Megan decided to move there, almost three thousand miles away. Though she didn't have a job when she arrived in Seattle, she soon found one as a producer at Microsoft.

A few years later, a friend introduced Megan to the CEO of Her Interactive, a studio you might remember from Brenda Laurel's chapter on page 37. At the time, Her Interactive was a branch of a larger company that was trying to, as the name implies, make games that appealed to women and girls. Though Megan wasn't a gamer and she didn't have any experience making games, she'd been telling stories for years, and she impressed Her Interactive so much that they hired her as a creative director. Her first project was one that instantly appealed to her: a *Nancy Drew* game. Megan had grown up reading the Nancy Drew books, and she wasn't about to pass up the chance to bring Nancy to life.

Just Make It Pink

You might remember this from earlier chapters, but just in case you don't, let's recap. During the mid-1990s, there was an incorrect but pervasive philosophy about what it meant to make games for young girls. It was an idea that stuck around like the most annoying wad of gum you've ever stepped in: *Just make the game pink.* If you were making a game for girls, all you needed to do was "slow down" mechanics used in other games, paint the plastic and box a bright pink, and blam, girl game.

Siiiiiiigh.

And hoo boy, was the Barbie brand of the 1980s and '90s pink. Like, it was *very pink.* I speak from experience: there were pink boxes, pink clothes, a pink mini-mansion, a pink convertible, and a pink cruise ship. Barbie even had a pink hot tub. Truly, she was living her best, pinkest life. Though it worked out well for Barbie, painting an entire demographic of people with the same (pink) brush is flawed and reductive, evidenced by Brenda Laurel's research and the launch of the Purple Games Movement. Like Brenda, Megan and the team at Her Interactive were experiencing a case of "Ugh, really?"

Her Interactive wanted to make games that were different from Barbie brand and style but still appealed to young girls—like the *Nancy Drew* books, a series of bestselling mystery novels. If *Nancy Drew* wasn't part of your childhood, or it's been a while, here's a quick refresher: Nancy is a young detective, between the ages of sixteen and eighteen, who solves mysteries. She's clever, determined, and curious, and her books don't talk down to their young audience. The first *Nancy Drew* book debuted in 1930, and *Nancy Drew* novels are still being written today, with every author who pens a *Nancy Drew* book calling themselves "Carolyn Keene." Nancy Drew is such an American staple that former Secretary of State Hillary Clinton and Supreme Court Justices Sandra Day O'Connor and Sonia Sotomayor have all listed *Nancy Drew* books as having a major impact on their lives.

Nancy Drew isn't pink. The book covers are often dark and moody, and the focus is on cleverness and adventure. If those books could appeal to young girls, Her Interactive was sure the games would, too. But designing games for an audience that hadn't played games before introduced its own set of challenges. The mechanics, story, and gameplay needed to be easy to learn but complex enough to keep players engaged.

Her Interactive ran regular playtests with girls between the ages of ten and fifteen, many of whom had never played a video game before. Being able to see the moments where they got stuck, lost, or frustrated helped the team make key adjustments, such as when one girl told them she thought Nancy was "too perfect." The team took the feedback seriously and rewrote Nancy to be more down-to-earth and have a sense of humor.

Even knowing the impact and popularity of the *Nancy Drew* books, the sales figures for the *Nancy Drew* games surprised Megan. The first game skyrocketed to success, and by 2021, the series had sold more than 9 million copies. It wasn't just little girls asking their parents to buy the games, but women who had grown up with the books playing and buying the game for themselves and their kids. "[People said] . . . just make the game pink, and they'll come," Megan said years later. "We decided to make it unpink, and they still came—in droves." After the *Nancy Drew* games debuted, *The New York Times* dubbed Her Interactive the "Un-Barbie of Computer Games."

A Leader at Heart

If her transition into making video games was abrupt, Megan's transition from creative director to CEO of Her Interactive was even more so. Quick breakdown: A CEO, or chief executive officer, is "the boss." The CEO is in charge of the department heads, who are in charge of the various creative and technical departments, which are full of people with specialties like 2D art or writing. You get the idea. To oversimplify, CEOs run a company, and they answer to the owners of that company.

In 1999, Her Interactive's board of directors met, and the CEO resigned. Okay, no big deal, right? The search might take a while, but the company would find a replacement eventually. Or immediately, as it turned out. Someone turned to Megan and said, "We think you could do it." Megan became CEO the same day.

Megan didn't have formal business training, and she didn't have any experience on the business side of things. What she did have was experience on teams. First, when she was a little girl playing baseball, tennis, softball, and hockey. Later, as creative director on *Nancy Drew*. She knew that treating her team as a collective of brilliant minds, rather than forcing her own views and opinions on everyone else, would make Her Interactive successful. "I was raised creatively," Megan said, "so I led that way." $8.5 million and nine million sold games later, that board member was proved right: Megan could do it. But first she'd have to find a way around retailers who assumed girls wouldn't buy games.

Nancy Drew Takes the Lead, Again

When Megan became CEO, Her Interactive had already worked on the *Nancy Drew* games, but despite the series' early success, a new obstacle stood between *Nancy Drew* and her players: distribution.

Distributors are the companies that sell video games to stores so they can be bought by gamers, and in the late 1990s and early 2000s, many of them refused to sell Her Interactive's games. They were convinced the *Nancy Drew* games wouldn't sell because of the narrative that girls and women didn't play video games. (Feel free to release that long sigh here.) So, Megan and her team had to figure out a workaround. At the time, Amazon.com was still pretty new, but Megan realized she could use it to sell Her Interactive's games directly to players, since the brick-and-mortar distributors wouldn't.

It worked. By 2003, *Nancy Drew* was the top adventure game franchise out there. The games' target audience turned out to be much, much wider than Megan or the team could have guessed. Not only were women between the ages of ten and eighty buying and enjoying the game, but gamers of other genders played it, too. *Nancy Drew* sold so well that Her Interactive ended up making thirty-two titles in the series, and Her Interactive took its place as the top creator of adventure-mystery games.

ERIN HOFFMAN

"My significant other works for Electronic Arts, and I'm what you might call a disgruntled spouse." So begins the EA spouse letter, as it has come to be called. It's a 2004 blog-post that criticizes the crunch and burnout all too common in the video game industry. Its author is Erin Hoffman, a gamedev and fantasy writer who worked on *DragonRealms* and *GoPets*. The letter was widely discussed by games journalists, designers, and business leaders and to this day, it remains one of the most memorable calls for better working conditions in the games industry.

Open-Minded and Open-Hearted

Of course, all good things must come to an end. Unless your name is Nancy Drew and people are still writing books, games, and comics about you, in which case you'll probably live forever. In 2013, Megan left Her Interactive to work on a variety of projects through her consulting group, Contagious Creativity, and she founded Leadership for Diversity (L4D) to teach others to lead as she did: creatively, disruptively, and successfully.

Though she stepped away from games to focus on multidisciplinary research and leadership training, Megan has never shied away from the industry or its difficult topics. Since leaving Her Interactive, she has spoken at conferences on everything from Gamergate to the—"Ugh, still? Really?"—pervasive idea that girls don't play games. In response to Gamergate, Megan said it should be a "wake-up call for the nation."

"Obviously we need more representation for women, ethnic diversity, LGBTQ, but the other thing we need is diverse thinkers," Megan said during a 2015 roundtable with *GamesBeat*. "Just because someone is a woman doesn't necessarily mean she's a diverse thinker. That's something we need to cultivate." It's a good reminder that diversity is about a lot more than gender, and learning constantly and changing the status quo to welcome more creators and gamers is something *we all* must do.

This, more than anything else, is what Megan points to when people ask about her success. She was willing to break rules and question conventional "wisdom," to make and sell the games no one else believed in—and she inspired an entire generation of young girls to do the same.

JANE JENSEN

The "interactive Anne Rice"

N O ONE, ABSOLUTELY no one, has logged as many hours playing *Gabriel Knight: Sins of the Fathers* as Jane Jensen. Okay, maybe someone has, but they can't be very far ahead of her. She's played the twentieth anniversary edition for fifty-seven hours, with 511 game saves, and she wrote the original *Gabriel Knight* game that shipped in 1993. After she and a team decided to re-release the game for its twentieth anniversary, Jane personally combed through every level and map to make sure the experience was perfect—hence, 511 game saves.

Gabriel Knight, a supernatural noir adventure game, was one of Sierra On-Line's most popular and beloved titles, and Jane is the reason why. She and the titular character actually have a lot in common, too. They both switched from a promising career to one that's way harder to explain at parties, and in doing so, they found their calling. Though, in Jane's case, there is less werewolf hunting. Hopefully.

A Quest for the King

Jane Jensen was born in 1963 in Palmerton, Pennsylvania, and from the time she was a little girl, she knew she wanted to be a writer. Even so, Jane knew that writing isn't the most stable of career paths, so when it was time for her to choose a field of study, she decided to major in computer science at Anderson University in Indiana.

Computer science courses taught Jane two important things about herself: One, that she loved logic puzzles and was quite good at them. Two, that she loved video games. Her first was *Colossal Cave Adventure* (the same one that inspired Roberta Williams, her future boss, to make *Mystery House*; see page 1). Still, it would take a few years for Jane to combine these interests into a career. In 1983, she was hired as a software engineer at Hewlett-Packard, a hardware-turned-computers company founded in a garage in 1939. By the time Jane joined, it was one of the biggest companies in Silicon Valley, California.

Though she was working with computers every day in college and at Hewlett-Packard, it wasn't until 1989 that Jane bought one for herself. Microcomputers, or computers that could fit onto someone's desk (as opposed to taking up a whole room—this is covered thoroughly in Joyce Weisbecker's chapter on page 98), crept onto the market in 1977. They gained popularity during the 1980s, when companies like Apple and IBM worked to make them more user-friendly to people without programming backgrounds. Gaming and business drove this success: people loved to play games, and computers made business communications and calculations faster and easier. In short, home computers weren't just a fad, but were becoming a household necessity.

When Jane joined the home-computer craze, she also bought a bunch of Sierra On-Line games. One of them, *King's Quest IV*, was written by the queen of adventure games herself,

Roberta Williams. Jane fell in love with the adventure genre, and she bought everything in Sierra's catalogue. Then she wrote to the studio. She sent her résumé and a short story she'd written, and she offered to do *any* job they would give her: programming, writing, quality assurance, whatever it took to work there.

She didn't hear back for nearly a year. When the call finally came, it was better news than Jane could've hoped for. Sierra was assembling, Nick Fury style, a "writers group" to help game designers create and keep track of things like story, setting, characters, dialogue, and progression. A hiring manager found Jane's résumé and thought she would be a good fit.

Working at Sierra meant Jane would have to move to Oakhurst, a California town three hours away from where she lived. Unlike her home in the Bay, Oakhurst was far away from pretty much everything: the ocean, the city, and the major highways. Plus, Jane would have to start in an entry-level role at Sierra, making less money than she did after six years as an engineer at Hewlett-Packard. All of this weighed on her as she tried to decide whether to take the job or stay where she was. Still, she agreed to interview with the company.

That interview settled Jane's mind: she knew she wanted to work for Sierra. "I didn't see a future in writing networking or operating system code the rest of my life," Jane told *Gamasutra* in 2007. "It bored the crap out of me." The interview showed Jane how much the people at Sierra enjoyed their work, and she wanted to be part of it. Whatever else they are, games—and their creation—are *never* boring.

The Queen's Protégé

If you read or watch interviews with former Sierra On-Line developers, you'll notice a common thread in the way they talk about the studio. They call it a career highlight, a collaborative workplace that was full of possibility. "It's definitely been eye-opening to realize how solid and stable Sierra was, and how supportive," Jane said in a Reddit AMA in 2015. "I don't think we appreciated it enough at the time, even though I loved working there."

Three years after playing *King's Quest* and discovering her love of adventure games, Jane co-wrote a *King's Quest* game with Roberta. A year later, she'd written or co-written three games and voice acted in another. Then she pitched her idea for *Gabriel Knight: Sins of the Fathers* to Ken, Roberta's husband. He was less than excited about the idea. This was a few years before Sierra released *Phantasmagoria* (which you might remember as Roberta's favorite game), and Ken had expected Jane to pitch a game more in-line with other titles in Sierra's canon: light-hearted, funny adventure games. *Gabriel Knight* would be anything but. It would be dark and dramatic and star flawed, complex characters.

Though Ken was unsure whether *Gabriel Knight* would be anything but a niche cult classic, both he and Roberta tried to give Sierra's designers as much creative freedom as possible. Ken greenlit the project and named Jane its director and lead writer. If it was a success, all of Sierra On-Line would celebrate with her. If it flopped, the blame would be hers alone.

Knight Takes Queen

Gabriel Knight: Sins of the Fathers is the story of, you guessed it, a guy named Gabriel Knight, a horror novelist and bookstore owner in New Orleans who investigates a series of supernatural murders. In 1993, Sierra On-Line released two versions of the game. One was stored on a floppy disk (a thin square of plastic and metal) and had no voice acting. The other was on CD-ROM (more plastic, but a round and shiny disc that could store way more data) and had voice acting. You might've heard of some of the actors, including Tim Curry, Leah Remini, and Mark Hamill. Yes, Luke Skywalker himself was in Jane's game.

Before we move on, it's important to note that there were both cons and pros with this game. One con is the game's setting: New Orleans. The city is home to rich and varied Haitian culture, which, unfortunately, is not well-represented in this game. A pro is Grace Nakimura, a major character in the series. She's a Japanese American researcher who, in the second and third *Gabriel Knight* games, becomes a playable character. She's eventually promoted to Gabriel's partner before leaving his side to pursue her own path as a supernatural investigator. As recently as 2013, games journalists have described Grace as one of the most well-rounded, realistic women characters in video games.

In 1993, *Sins of the Fathers* swept the gaming landscape. *Computer Gaming World Magazine* named it Adventure Game of the Year in 1994 (alongside *Day of the Tentacle*— they were both so good, they had to share). The magazine also gave the game's narrator, Broadway star and TV actress Virginia Capers, the award for Best Female Voice-Over Acting and dubbed Jane "the interactive Anne Rice" (you might remember her from Amy Briggs's chapter, page 83). Jane chose to take this comparison a step further: she adapted the *Gabriel Knight* games into novels while she was still working on the games. In 1997, she released a novelization of *Sins of the Father*, followed by an adaptation of the second game in 1998.

The third and final game, *Gabriel Knight 3: Blood of the Sacred, Blood of the Damned*, shipped in 1999, after Ken and Roberta Williams had sold Sierra. Jane left the company the same year. Sierra On-Line just wasn't the same without the people who had founded it, and though Jane had become one of its most prolific and well-regarded game directors, it was time to move on.

In all, Jane made three games in the *Gabriel Knight* series. All three were praised by critics for their dark tone and beautiful prose, and they earned a devoted fan base as well as regularly appear in lists and bundles of the "Best Sierra Games."

Looking Past the Knight

Gabriel Knight is probably Jane's best-known work, but it's far from the only thing she's created. She's an award-nominated novelist who has written more than forty books, including more than twenty under the pen name Eli Easton. Jane's directed, written, consulted, and helped design seventeen more games, which range from Agatha Christie mysteries to a globe-trotting, artifact-hunting adventure called *Moebius*. She cofounded mobile studios Oberon Games and Pinkerton Road, and she has been featured in the National Women's History Museum and the The Strong National Museum of Play. In addition to all this, when she published a new *Gabriel Knight* story in 2014, it made a lot of headlines.

And it all happened because Jane wrote a moody, complex mystery at a time when many, even Roberta Williams's husband, thought games needed to stick to light stories. Jane became "the interactive Anne Rice" because she didn't make the games people expected— she made the games *she wanted to play*.

LINDA CURRIE

The gamer in the family

T HE HIGH SCHOOL girls' bathroom is a prominent feature in many teen movies and YA novels: a place of drama, secrets, crushes, and, presumably, secret crushes. It's not, typically, where teenage girls go find jobs in game development. But maybe it should be. The year was 1981, and Linda Sirotek was in the girls' bathroom asking around for a non-menthol cigarette. Brenda Romero, as you might remember from her chapter on page 108, had one. The two started talking, and the rest, as they say, is history.

1-800-Linda-Help Me Win

Before we talk about Linda and Brenda's meeting in the girls' bathroom, we have to go back to 1979 and talk about two brothers from Massachusetts. They and their father decided to do what all the cool kids of the 1970s and '80s were doing: they cofounded a game studio. Well, a software company that made games on the side. Sirotech Software's first game, released in 1980, was called *Galactic Attack* and was about starships, strategy, and phasers. The following year, the family rebranded Sirotech as Sir-Tech, and the brothers teamed up with two more developers to make a 1981 fantasy game called *Wizardry: Proving Grounds of the Mad Overlord* for the Apple II computer.

This is where the story takes a fun twist. Though the brothers were avid coders and developers, they didn't play their own game very much—but their sister did. Linda Sirotek (before she married and became Linda Currie), then fifteen years old, loved *Wizardry*'s dark hallways, heavy footsteps, and the big letters that warned AN ENCOUNTER before you faced a monster. She couldn't get enough of the game, and before long, she knew it even better than the people who had made it.

We already covered this in Brenda Romero's chapter, but a quick refresher is in order. These were the days before walkthroughs and online hints for video games, so Sir-Tech decided to start a tip line that players could call for help if they got stuck. Because Linda loved playing *Wizardry*, she seemed like the obvious fit to run the tip line. At fifteen years old, she was working her first gamedev job, a mishmash of quality assurance, support, and community engagement. That job eventually passed to Brenda.

After high school, Linda worked as a tester on the next three *Wizardry* games while she studied economics and marketing at the Wharton School of Business. She graduated in 1988 and kept working in games, but didn't make them her full-time job until 1994, when her family asked her to launch Sir-Tech's Canadian branch. Around the same time, Linda met the man she would eventually marry. Ian Currie was the creator of the *Jagged Alliance* series, and the two became a game-design power couple. But the standout game in Linda's career was yet to come.

Wizards, Wizards Everywhere

The *Wizardry* series gained a passionate following throughout the 1990s, and in '96, Linda's Canadian branch began work on the eighth installment in the series. Fans were thrilled.

Then a year passed. And another. And another. Keep in mind, this was the era when games generally took a year or so to make, so fans began to wonder: What is taking so long?

As is often the case in gamedev, the culprit was technology. The *Wizardry 8* team (on which, you might remember, Brenda Romero worked as a designer and writer) wanted the game to play like a modern RPG, which meant adding things Sir-Tech had never tried before: voiceover performances, 3D models, updated graphics, and a more intuitive user interface. That meant switching programming languages, which added a year to the project, and overhauling their entire engine.

> ⇒ User interface, or UI, is how information is presented to the player. Menus, button presses, and health bars are all part of a UI scheme. They can be diegetic, meaning they appear in the fiction of the game, like Ellie's map in *The Last of Us 2*, or non-diegetic, meaning they aren't part of the game's fictional setting, like the health bar in *Street Fighter*.

Wizardry 8 spent about five years in production. While the result might have taken longer than anyone on the team wanted, fans were so impressed with the game, they didn't complain. *Wizardry 8* was many game magazines' and critics' "RPG of the Year." Sixteen years after it shipped, *IGN* named it one of the greatest RPGs of all time. The turn-based, party-building dungeon crawler was exactly what players craved, and the depth of design had them hooked.

Linda's family had created the peak of the *Wizardry* experience—and, sadly, it would be the last game in the series.

The Beginning of the End

Despite the success of the *Wizardry* and the *Jagged Alliance* series, Sirtech Canada was in financial trouble. The relatively small company had to compete against publishing juggernauts like Electronic Arts and Nintendo, and they were falling behind. In 1998, the American branch of Sir-Tech gave up the fight and closed its doors, though Linda's Canadian branch remained open. "We just don't think that the future, at least in the next three or five years, bodes very well for independents," Linda's brother Robert told *IGN* the same year they shut the doors. He believed small and mid-level studios would start to vanish or be taken over by major publishers, and that fewer, less-innovative games—"safe" games, as they're sometimes called—would dominate the industry going forward.

Wizardry 8 might have seemed like the savior Sirtech Canada needed, but even its success wasn't enough to keep the lights on. Two years after the game shipped, Sirtech Canada shut down, as well.

Though the studio was gone, Linda was not, and she had twenty-two years of experience in games that other studios were eager to put to use. She was a designer and producer for *Zoo Tycoon 2* and its DLC, then became a creative director at Creat Studios. She was named design director at Turbine in 2010. It wasn't until 2012, after Linda had been in games for thirty-one years, that she left the industry for good.

In every sense of the word, Linda Currie is one of the early builders who created the games industry as we know it today. Her work on *Wizardry* and at Sirtech built a foundation that went on to inspire other gamedevs, including Brenda Romero. She was a builder, designer, gamer, businesswoman, and gamedev, and one of the reasons RPGs and games look and play the way they do today.

SHERI GRANER RAY

The conversation stopper (and starter)

A GROUP OF DUDES are clustered in a loose blob. They're convention attendees, and they're most likely talking about games, panels, or possibly where to get the best coffee (if they're in San Francisco, it's Sightglass; don't fight me). Then a woman walks up to the group, and the conversation dies. They know who she is, and they know that if any of them have put something sexist or misogynistic in their games, they're about to hear about it. She's going to ask them *why* they did it, and she's going to make them *defend* their reasoning. This woman is Sheri Graner Ray, thirty-year game design veteran, founder of Women in Games International, and author of *Gender Inclusive Game Design*.

"I know for a while there I gained kind of a stigma in the industry of being difficult to work with because of it," Sheri said in a 2012 *NYMG Feminist Game Studies* podcast. "I don't think I was difficult to work with, but I would continually ask, but 'what if your player is female?'" It's a question teams should be asking themselves, and until they do, Sheri won't stop—even if having to answer makes people uncomfortable. *Especially* then.

The DM Becomes the Designer

Growing up in McAllen, Texas, Sheri wasn't surrounded by comic book shops, arcades, or computers. She wasn't particularly drawn to technology, but she loved playing pretend with her friends, and she was an endlessly creative performer. In high school, she was a competitive ventriloquist who won district and state competitions. "Who knows," she quipped in a 2018 interview with the IGDA, "maybe a second career for me on cruise ships, eh?"

No wonder, then, that when *Dungeons & Dragons* started to soar in popularity in the late 1970s and early '80s, Sheri ran to the game with open arms. She became a dungeon master, also called a DM, who plays as the narrator of the game. The DM voices every NPC in the world, runs the combat for every antagonist, and designs every puzzle, map, and obstacle. The DM's first and most important role is to "run the game." It's a *lot* like the job of a game writer or narrative designer, so it's no wonder so many of us (including yours truly) found our love for narrative design playing *D&D*.

Sheri's hobby began to slide toward a career in 1989, when she attended a game conference and ran a *D&D* session for her friends. Another conference attendee was looking for a group to play with, so Sheri's friends invited him to their table. He had so much fun that he kept playing with Sheri's group in the months after the conference. Oh, and this is important: he worked for a company called Origin Systems, a studio in Austin, Texas. A few months after joining Sheri's *D&D* group, he told her, "Sheri, you write all your own stuff, you design all your own modules and adventures for this group. I kind of think you're a natural fit for the company I work for, and they're looking for a writer right now. Do you want to put in your résumé?" She did, more out of curiosity than because she thought she'd get the job. Within a month, she was hired.

Sheri worked at Origin while she was attending college at St. Edward's University in Austin, Texas. While it was a dream job in terms of the work—crafting plot lines, rule sets, and character—the deadlines created a mess of chronic overtime and crunch (you might remember the crunch callout in the "EA spouse letter" penned by Erin Hoffman, page 116). Sheri was juggling English and creative writing classes while working twelve-plus-hour days seven days per week. Management eventually let up *somewhat*; they gave the devs Sundays off. "So we could do laundry," Sheri told me. Cue the exasperated groan.

This would become something of a theme in Sheri's career. She loved the work itself, but the culture in and around gamedev teams and publishers had problems. Even when she was young and new to the industry, Sheri didn't hesitate to call them out.

Never Give Up, Never Surrender

The first time Sheri spoke out was when Origin began work on a game called *Arthurian Legends*. The player-character was a Knight of the Round Table, one of the warriors sworn to the mythical King Arthur of England. While there are no women knights in the stories of King Arthur, there are a lot of strong, powerful, and complex women characters, including Morgana Le Fay, the Lady of the Lake, and Guinevere. Regardless, the team decided that there wouldn't be any female knights in the game. When the studio pitched the game to the design team, which included Sheri, she asked what she felt was the obvious question, "What if the player's a woman?"

It became something of a joke at Origin. If someone pitched an idea, Sheri would follow up by asking, "What if the player's a woman?" At first, the question was greeted with a smile, sometimes a shrug. Then a frown. Then a cold shoulder. The design team stopped inviting Sheri to meetings. If you're thinking, "Wow, that sounds really childish," that's because it is. Sheri would look up from her desk, realize all the other designers were gone, and be forced to play, in her words, Hunt the Game Design Meeting.

Sheri doesn't often talk about "war stories," as she calls them, the times when people have said or done rude, belittling, or sexist things to her. The reason? Those stories spark anger at one individual, or maybe a few, but they rarely turn into meaningful action. In her opinion, it's far more useful to talk about the successes and shifts *the industry* has gone through in the way it treats marginalized people, rather than spend her time focusing on a few individuals.

A few years ago, the International Game Developers Association asked Sheri, "What's the best advice anyone's ever given you?" "Never give up. Never surrender." Captain Nesmith, *Galaxy Quest*. If there's one way to sum up Sheri's advocacy, it would be that phrase.

Inclusive Design

Sometimes it is hard to remember that the video game industry is still somewhat young, at least compared with film and the printing press. Fifteen years often feel like a hundred in the world of game development (see: how PlayStation 5 games look compared to PlayStation 3 games). Because of this, and because of the intensity of the creative work and long hours, it isn't uncommon to hear about game developers leaving the industry long before they retire. They switch to jobs in marketing, film, oyster farming, you name it. Okay, I have no proof someone gave up game design to be an oyster farmer, but that doesn't mean it didn't happen. The point is, gamedevs with ten years of experience are considered rare, wonderful, wise gemstones. Fifteen? *Whoa.* Twenty? Please give us your secrets of time travel, Time Lord. And then there's Sheri, clocking in at a cool thirty-plus years. Even the Time Lords are impressed.

In her thirty years as a game designer, she's written and designed games like *Ultima*, *Star Wars Galaxies*, and *Nancy Drew* (which you probably remember from Megan Gaiser's chapter on page 112). She's worked at Sony, Electronic Arts, Cartoon Network, and even with the US Department of Defense on an educational game. Her games are known for their thoughtful attention to detail and weaving interactive storytelling with writing.

Outside of her direct work on games, Sheri's become known for the attention she's given to the industry and its culture. After Sheri had been in games for about fifteen years, she published her first book, *Gender Inclusive Game Design: Expanding the Market*. The 2004 book challenged the idea that men and boys should be treated as the baseline demographic for games. You might remember this as the same argument that other iconic women gamedevs have been making for a while, including Keiko Erikawa (page 30) and Brenda Laurel (page 37). Sheri didn't just point out the obvious—that, yes, women play and make games. Instead, she separated out player types and goals, and she gave advice on how to design games that appealed to different groups of people based on their *preferences*, not just their *demographics*. Sheri started a conversation that would continue for more than a decade. Because of her book and research, further study has been done into what motivates diverse sets of players, and in 2005, she won the IGDA Award for Community Contribution at the Game Developers Choice Awards.

Today, Sheri is still designing games, and she remains a passionate advocate for women who want to enter the industry as players, streamers, and developers. She's particularly excited about the indie game movement and the emergence of college and graduate game design majors. Her hope is that game design programs will pull in developers who are diverse not just by gender, but racially and culturally as well. More perspectives, she continues to argue, mean better games, better art, and better audiences.

To that end, Sheri cofounded Women in Games International (WiGI) in 2005, one of the largest and most well-known advocacy groups in games. The group, which counts people of many genders among its members, pushes not only for more inclusivity in games, but offers the training and guidance to make it happen. "We really need to do quite a bit of outreach and let [girls] see women in industry, let them see role models," Sheri said in the 2012 *NYMG* podcast. "So we can say, 'look: there is a place for girls in games. And we want you here.'"

Sheri wants marginalized people to know that the uphill climb isn't all there is to game development. There's joy and passion, too. She loves to build worlds and characters from nothing, to breathe life into them and create an experience guided by the player. There is no other medium like it, and Sheri loves it enough that she's stuck with video games through the hard times and cold shoulders. She wants every aspiring gamedev to know it's a field worth pursuing, no matter who you are. And she wants to build an entire industry willing to ask the hard questions, so more of us can be the conversation stoppers and starters.

CONSTANCE STEINKUEHLER

In 2011, US President Barack Obama appointed a senior expert to advise him on video games and their influence on culture and education. That expert was Constance Steinkuehler. She teaches informatics and studies everything from online fandoms to learning labs. She's also studied how students learn while playing video games. Her goal? To use the same methods that make games engaging to help kids pay attention in school. Constance and Mabel Addis Mergardt probably would've gotten along famously.

ELONKA DUNIN

The gamedev-slash-code-cracker

THE YEAR WAS 2000, and someone handed game designer Elonka Dunin a flier printed with the PhreakNIC Code. To anyone who isn't a code breaker, the PhreakNIC Code looks like a meaningless jumble of symbols, numbers, and letters. To Elonka and crypto experts like her, it looked like a challenge. When Elonka discovered the puzzle, it had been circulated for a year, and no one had managed to break it. Curious, Elonka wanted to try—and she broke it in ten days.

That's how, in 2003, Elonka found herself in the halls of the US government. She was brought in to teach cryptography to a group trying to decipher Al Qaeda's codes. Just like that, Elonka had gone from game designer to international crypto authority.

Puzzles on Paper

Elonka can't remember a time when puzzles *didn't* fascinate her. When she was barely old enough to walk, her mother could leave her on a porch with a puzzle, and Elonka would play for hours. When she was a little older, she started playing tabletop games, such as the space exploration game *Galaxy*, at her dining room table with her father and his friends. Around the same time, one of Elonka's neighbors began studying code breaking to earn his Boy Scout merit badge. She visited his house constantly, peppering him with questions until he finally handed over every book he owned on cryptography. Elonka's lifelong passion was born.

She was born in 1958 in Santa Monica, California, the daughter of two graduates from the University of California Los Angeles who would later teach there. Her father, Stanley, taught engineering and mathematics, and her mother, Elsie, taught dance and ethnology, which is the comparative study of cultures. Stanley was born in Warsaw, Poland, and was orphaned at a young age by the events of World War II. One of his aunts, a Catholic Auschwitz survivor, took Stanley and his sisters to France, and with the help of another uncle, she brought them to the United States when Stanley was a teenager. Stanley became a programmer as well as a teacher, and he worked on everything from NASA projects, such as the world's first geosynchronous communications satellite to stock brokerages and the title insurance industry.

⟹ "Geosynchronous" means Earth-centered and in sync with the time it takes the Earth to rotate on its axis: 23 hours, 56 minutes, and 4 seconds.

Throughout his variety of work, one constant remained: Elonka, his young daughter, who often tagged along with him. She sat in rooms filled wall to wall and floor to ceiling with giant mainframe computers. None of this was the norm for people in the 1960s and '70s. For starters, most didn't have access to a mainframe computer, and home computers

wouldn't become popular until the 1980s. To keep his daughter entertained, Stanley programmed simple number games she could play on the computers. She played these as well as *Colossal Cave Adventure*, *Dungeon*, and games created by college computer science and programming students, such as the *Star Trek* games of the 1970s. As Elonka grew older, she learned to program her own games.

As she learned to tinker with games on mainframe computers, her middle school—which didn't own a single computer—began teaching her to code by hand, filling in dots on a punch card with #2 pencils. Those cards were then mailed to a downtown facility, where the dots were punched, and the card was fed into a mainframe computer. A day or two later, the students received "debugging printouts" back to see how their code worked. The turnaround time for debugging a line of code could take an entire week as opposed to the seconds it takes now.

Elonka graduated from high school in 1976 and started taking classes at UCLA though she wasn't sure what she wanted to study, so she chose astronomy. It didn't quite click, so a year later, she dropped out of college to join the United States Air Force. In the military, she was asked to select a career path, but Elonka still wasn't sure what she wanted to do. The Air Force sent her wherever she was most needed, and at the time, that meant avionics instrumentation. She worked on the dials, transmitters, and wiring used by pilots and copilots. She was moved from California to the United Kingdom, then back to California, to work on tankers, cargo jets, spy planes, and more.

However, she wasn't, in her own words, "really stellar" at the job. Through it all, her interest in computers never waned, so she asked to switch to a job that involved them, but the military was reluctant to cross-train her. They needed more avionics specialists than programmers, and they didn't want her to switch roles. Elonka stayed in the military two years longer than her original enlistment period, hoping she would be able to switch jobs, but when it didn't happen, she left without any regrets. "Oh well," she wrote later on her blog, "their loss!"

Elonka picked up a lot in the military: discipline, time management, and a love for *Dungeons & Dragons*. While she was stationed at RAF Mildenhall in Suffolk, England, she became known as the base's "Dungeon Mistress," running games in the community center. Around the same time, she started playing games on her coworkers' microcomputers. One of them had a TRS-80, another a Commodore, and Elonka finally bought her own, an Osborne. She started programming games as she'd once done on mainframes, writing them in BASIC, and she bought games like *Fool's Errand*, *Ultima*, and *Wizardry*. In particular, BBS (or bulletin board system) games like *Scepter* and *British Legends* caught Elonka's attention.

> ⟶ "BASIC" is the name of the programming language, not any judgment call on whether it's basic or complicated. It stands for "Beginners' All-purpose Symbolic Instruction Code."

Multiplayer games were still new on the gaming scene, led by people like Danielle Bunten Berry (page 68) in the 1980s, but Danielle's multiplayer games required multiple people gathered around one machine. BBS games were remote, running on shared servers connected by phone lines and dial-up modems—this was before the internet linked computers and consoles seamlessly.

After she left the military, Elonka worked at a series of temp secretary jobs for law firms while she figured out what she wanted to do next. On the side, she kept playing every computer game she could find, and she later wrote on her website, "My journals from the era are filled with notes critiquing every game, comparing difficulty of various puzzles, trying out different solution techniques, and recording my successes for beating each game in turn."

Eventually, she found an online service called GEnie and a game called *GemStone*, a high-fantasy role-playing game and one of the first MMORPGs ever created. Elonka was instantly hooked, writing, "I tore through that game, learning it so fast that the other players were convinced that I must be a 'reroll'—an older player who was pretending to be a new one." Seriously, Elonka was so good, people were convinced she must be cheating. "But no, I just loved the game." She got so good at it, in fact, that in 1989, Simutronics, the studio behind *GemStone*, asked Elonka to be one of *GemStone III*'s first beta testers. That opportunity led her to a convention, where she met the devs. They hit it off so well that soon, Elonka was packing her bags and moving from Los Angeles to St. Louis, Missouri, to work at the studio.

She didn't have a college degree or a lengthy computer science–heavy résumé, but she had determination, passion, and a hobby she'd loved enough to make into a career—three traits that would serve Elonka time and time again in the years to come.

Cracking the Code

Within a year of joining Simutronics, Elonka was running *GemStone III*. She worked in a variety of roles—product manager, technical writer, and executive producer—on games like *CyberStrike*, *Hercules & Xena*, *Modus Operandi*, and *DragonRealms*. With all of her experience in online gaming, it's no wonder Dragon Con invited her to speak at the convention in 2000.

Elonka had been making video games professionally for ten years when JonnyX, the organizer of a hacker convention in Nashville, created a version of the PhreakNIC Code for convention attendees. No one was able to crack it. So JonnyX handed out fliers with the code printed on it and promised whoever managed to break it an all-expense-paid trip to a hacker con. Elonka found one of these fliers at Dragon Con and took it with her when she went home.

A week after Dragon Con, Elonka was sick with what many of us not-so-lovingly call the "con crud," the illness you inevitably catch after you've spent time with thousands of people in crowded convention halls. Elonka was its latest victim, so she had time to kill while recuperating. Solving the puzzle felt like a good way to pass the time. "I got pretty obsessed with it," she wrote later. The code was all she talked about, and she looked up discussion archives online of people discussing the code itself. Ten days later, she cracked it.

Elonka vs. Kryptos

Outside the Central Intelligence Agency headquarters in Virginia, there is a twelve-foot-tall sculpture, a curved slab of copper covered in bold block letters. These letters form four separate puzzles, of which three have been solved. The fourth, however, remains one of the most famous unsolved codes in the world. Even Elonka hasn't solved it—yet. She's not done trying.

After she broke the PhreakNIC Code, Elonka published books and articles on cryptography, was interviewed on radio and television, and came to be a well-known expert in the field. Ever heard of a book called *The Lost Symbol*? Or what about *The Da Vinci Code*? Both were written by Dan Brown, and Elonka helped him research the codes and puzzles he wanted to include in the books (it's kind of Dan Brown's thing). To thank her, he named a character in *The Lost Symbol* Nola Kaye, an anagrammed version of Elonka's name.

As this book goes to print, Elonka hasn't solved Kryptos, but she's become such a well-known expert on it that when the sculptor himself, Jim Sanborn, decided to tell the public about an error he'd made on the sculpture, he reached out to Elonka. She was the one he chose to make the announcement about the error and explain the ramifications—that's how much he trusted her.

Just like the toddler on the porch playing with a puzzle for hours, or the little girl coding her own games on a mainframe, Elonka had discovered a challenge and thrown herself into it wholeheartedly. She is determined to solve the unsolvable. And why wouldn't she? The PhreakNIC Code was unbreakable, too—until she broke it.

JANET MURRAY

SIDE QUEST

The similarities between theater and games have come up several times in this book, but in 1997, Janet Murray decided to turn that concept into *Hamlet on the Holodeck: The Future of Narrative in Cyberspace*, one of the most important academic works about video games. The central question of Janet's book was whether a computer could become an expressive method of storytelling, just as the stage is one for the theater. This isn't a totally new idea, and if you've ever read the 1953 book *Fahrenheit 451* or the 1932 novel *Brave New World*, you know that many authors view "cyber-escapism" as a symptom of a dystopian society. Janet takes a different view, the same shared by the *Star Trek* universe (hence, the holodeck): that games and cyber-stories can help humans educate and entertain one another, as stories always have. Also, because video games are interactive, they can teach people important things about themselves.

TO QUOTE ROBIN HUNICKE, "WHAT'S NEXT?"

SPOILERS: IT'S MORE than hot chicks.

The IGDA Developer Satisfaction Survey is one of the best sources of industry demographics and trends. In 2019, the survey reported that women still made up less than a quarter of game developers in the industry. The number gets worse for female-identifying people of color: of respondents to the survey, 81 percent were white, an overwhelming majority that indicates clear racial bias.

However, the future isn't bleak or hopeless. Far from it. But it does mean that there is still a lot of work to be done. Since that IGDA report was released, the number of women game designers has gone up and continues to rise. In the same study, 61 percent of game developers said diversity is "very important." Groups like Women in Games International, Women in Games Jobs, and the IGDA's Women in Games Special Interest Group work to include and train women in the industry. The IGDA's Black in Games, Latinx in Games, and I Need Diverse Games support communities and growth for game developers of color. All these groups share one message: "We are here making games, and we belong here."

Women have been speaking out about their place and treatment in the games industry since the 1980s. Many of these fights go back even further, when women were making inroads in engineering, programming, multimedia, virtual reality, and dot-com companies. The difference now is the platform. Women have more avenues than ever to express themselves: on social media, blogs, and gaming news websites. It's not a perfect win, but it's a win.

I hope this book has inspired you to chase your passion, whether it's in video game development or elsewhere. As you begin creating, remember to promote yourself and people of color, transgender men and women, nonbinary people, those who speak a different language than you, people from different countries, people from different cultures, and so many more. Art has never been made by one gender, one race, one country, or one religious group: it comes from all corners of the world. So do video games.

I won't say there aren't difficult days as a game designer. I won't say that misogyny and harassment are things of the past, because they're not. I certainly won't give a pass to the people, cultures, and practices that have driven talented women from the games industry. However, there is so much more to game production than just the negative things. In writing this book, I hoped to show that people of many genders and backgrounds built these operas out of bridges, and *nothing*, not cruelty or harassment or jealousy, can take that away.

You might not remember every name, studio, and game featured in this book, and that's okay. What I hope you do remember is this: A profound sense of joy and purpose. The knowledge that there is work to be done in this beautiful, messy field, and that you could be part of it. I hope this book dispels your fear. I hope you see a future that is growing brighter with every new developer who decides to make games. And I hope you realize that developer could be *you*.

A LIST OF SOURCES AND ADDITIONAL READING, IF YOU JUST
CAN'T GET ENOUGH.

Roberta Williams

Cox, Angela R. "Women by Women: A Gender Analysis of Sierra Titles by Women
Designers." *Feminism in Play*, 2018, 21–35, doi: 10.1007/978-3-319-90539-6_2.

Drumm, Perrin. "Roberta Williams Is the World's First Graphic Computer Game Designer—
But She's Famous for All the Wrong Reasons." *Eye on Design*, March 11, 2020,
https://eyeondesign.aiga.org/roberta-williams-is-the-worlds-first-graphic-computer
-game-designer-but-shes-famous-for-all-the-wrong-reasons/.

Givens, Linda Holden. "Williams, Roberta Lynn (b. 1953)." HistoryLink.org, November 11, 2019,
www.historylink.org/File/20912.

Nooney, Laine. "Let's Begin Again: Sierra On-Line and the Origins of the Graphical Adventure
Game." *American Journal of Play*. November 30, 2016, https://eric.ed.gov/?id=EJ1166784.

Nooney, Laine. "The Odd History of the First Erotic Computer Game." *The Atlantic*,
May 15, 2018, www.theatlantic.com/technology/archive/2014/12
/the-odd-history-of-the-first-erotic-computer-game/383114/.

Nooney, Laine. "The Uncredited: Work, Women, and the Making of the U.S. Computer Game
Industry." *Feminist Media Histories* 6, no. 1 (2020): 119–146, doi: 10.1525/fmh.2020.6.1.119.

Petit, Carolyn, and Anita Sarkeesian. "Gender Breakdown of Games Featured at E3 2019."
Feminist Frequency, November 18, 2020, https://feministfrequency.com/2019/06/14
/gender-breakdown-of-games-featured-at-e3-2019/.

"Roberta Williams." Lemelson, https://lemelson.mit.edu/resources/roberta-williams.

Muriel Tramis

Baker, Chris. "How 'French Touch' Gave Early Videogames Art, Brains." *Wired*, Conde Nast,
June 4, 2010, www.wired.com/2010/06/french-touch-games/.

Chang, Alenda Y. "Une Vie Bien Jouée / A Life Well Played: The Cultural Legacy of Game
Designer Muriel Tramis." *Feminist Media Histories*, vol. 6, no. 1, Jan. 2020, pp. 147–162, doi:
https://doi.org/10.1525/fmh.2020.6.1.147.

Chilton, Maddi. "A Forgotten, Decades-Old Game About Slavery Has Returned."
Kill Screen, June 1, 2016, killscreen.com/previously/articles/can-now-play-decades
-old-forgotten-game-slavery/.

Choppin, Damien. "On Vous Présente Muriel Tramis, Pionnière Du Jeu Vidéo Et Première Femme
Du Secteur à Recevoir La Légion D'honneur." *Business Insider France*, October 25, 2018.

Jankowski, Filip. "Political and Social Issues in French Digital Games, 1982–1993."
TransMissions: The Journal of Film and Media Studies, vol. 2, no. 2, 2017, pp. 162–176.

Jankowski, Filip. "The Presence of Female Designers in French Video Game Industry, 1985–1993."
   Games and Culture, vol. 15, no. 6, 2019, pp. 670–684, doi: 10.1177/1555412019841954.

Lee, Elijah. "A First Lady of Gaming: The First Black Female Game Designer." *The Icon*,
   March 4, 2021, www.theicon.com/a-first-lady-of-gaming/.

Salvador, Phil. "Muriel Tramis Speaks about Her Career and the Memory of Martinique."
   The Obscuritory, March 5, 2018, obscuritory.com/essay/muriel-tramis-interview/.

Taylor, Hadyn. "Muriel Tramis Becomes Second-Ever Game Designer Awarded the Legion
   of Honour." *GamesIndustry.biz*, July 19, 2018, www.gamesindustry.biz/articles/2018-07-19
   -muriel-tramis-becomes-second-ever-game-designer-awarded-the-legion-of-honor.

Woitier, Chloé. "Pionnière Du Jeu Vidéo En France, Muriel Tramis Reçoit La Légion D'honneur."
   LEFIGARO, October 26, 2018, www.lefigaro.fr/medias/2018/10/26/20004
   -20181026ARTFIG00157-pionniere-du-jeu-video-en-france-muriel-tramis-recoit
   -la-legion-d-honneur.php.

Wolf, Mark J. P. *Video Games Around the World*. MIT Press, 2015.

Dona Bailey

Alexander, Leigh. "The Original Gaming Bug: Centipede Creator Dona Bailey."
   Gamasutra, August 27, 2007, www.gamasutra.com/view/feature/130082/the_original
   _gaming_bug_centipede_.php.

Bailey, Dona. "r/IAmA—I Am Dona Bailey, Former Atari Programmer of Arcade Centipede,
   Unix Programmer, Linux Teacher, Adobe CS Teacher, Rhetoric and Writing University
   Professor, Lifelong Learner, Big Reader. I'm Here to Answer Any Questions. AMA!"
   Reddit, February 16, 2017, www.reddit.com/r/IAmA/comments/5ugvqv/i_am_dona_bailey
   _former_atari_programmer_of/.

Chess, Shira. *Ready Player Two: Women Gamers and Designed Identity*. University of
   Minnesota Press, 2017.

"Dona Bailey." *Atari Women*, March 8, 2019, www.atariwomen.org/stories/dona-bailey/.

Foxx-Gonzalez, Kellie. "Meet Dona Bailey, The Woman Behind Atari's Centipede."
   The Mary Sue, July 10, 2012, www.themarysue.com/donna-bailey-centipede/.

Marie, Meagan. *Women in Gaming: 100 Professionals of Play*. Prima Games, an Imprint of
   Random House LLC, 2018.

Ortutay, Barbara. "Woman Behind 'Centipede' Recalls Game Icon's Birth." *Yahoo!
   Finance*, Yahoo!, June 30, 2012, finance.yahoo.com/news/woman-behind-centipede
   -recalls-game-213543658.html.

Porges, Seth. "The Happy Accidents That Led To The Arcade Classic 'Centipede.'"
   Forbes, November 30, 2017, www.forbes.com/sites/sethporges/2017/11/30
   /the-happy-accidents-that-led-to-the-arcade-classic-centipede/#2b80f9902e46.

Rouse, Richard. "Chapter 6: Interview: Ed Logg." *Game Design: Theory and Practice* (2nd Edition).
   Jones & Bartlett Learning, 2004.

Salen, Katie, and Eric Zimmerman. *The Game Design Reader: A Rules of Play Anthology*.
   MIT Press, 2009.

Suellentrop, Chris. "Saluting the Women Behind the Screen." *The New York Times*,
August 19, 2014, www.nytimes.com/2014/08/20/arts/video-games/those
-underappreciated-female-video-game-pioneers.html.

Yates, Chelsea. "Atari Women." *UW College of Engineering*, December 27, 2019,
www.engr.washington.edu/news/article/2019-07-15/atari-women.

Kazuko Shibuya

Agossah, Iyane. "Final Fantasy Pixel Artist Kazuko Shibuya Comments on Her Career
and the JRPG Series' Early Days." *DualShockers*, July 5, 2019, www.dualshockers.com
/kazuko-shibuya-final-fantasy-japan-expo/.

Audureau, William. "Kazuko Shibuya, La Reine Des Pixels Des Premiers 'Final Fantasy.'"
Le Monde.fr, Le Monde, July 9, 2019, www.lemonde.fr/pixels/article/2019/07/09/kazuko
-shibuya-la-reine-des-pixels-des-premiers-final-fantasy_5487205_4408996.html.

Burnham, Van. *Supercade: A Visual History of the Videogame Age 1971–1984*. MIT Press, 2003.

Friscia, John. "Final Fantasy Artist Talks about Early Days of Square & Final Fantasy."
Nintendo Enthusiast, Nintendo Enthusiast, July 5, 2019, www.nintendoenthusiast.com
/final-fantasy-artist-kazuko-shibuya-square-early-days-pixel-art/.

Ogura, Masaya. "Kazuko Shibuya—Square Developer Interview." *4gamer.Net*, March 2013,
www.4gamer.net/games/064/G006480/20130227073/.

Robin Hunicke

"Burn Baby, Burn: Game Developers Rant." *GDC Vault*, www.gdcvault.com/play/1013249
/Burn-Baby-Burn-Game-Developers.

Games for Change. "Keynote—Designing Future Realities with Robin Hunicke."
YouTube video, 35:38, August 2, 2019, www.youtube.com/watch?v=l7D5GCV1
-kM&ab_channel=GamesforChange.

Plessis, Corné Du. "Subverting Utilitarian Subject-Object Relations in Video Games:
A Philosophical Analysis of thatgamecompany's Journey." *South African Journal of
Philosophy*, vol. 37, no. 4, 2018, pp. 466–479, doi: 10.1080/02580136.2018.1532189.

Stuart, Keith. "Robin Hunicke on Journey, AI and Games That Know They're Games." *The
Guardian*, December 6, 2011, www.theguardian.com/technology/gamesblog/2011/dec/06
/journey-preview-robin-hunicke-interview.

Takahashi, Dean. "UC Santa Cruz Taps Journey Co-Creator Robin Hunicke to Teach
Game Development." *VentureBeat*, October 14, 2014, venturebeat.com/2014/10/14
/uc-santa-cruz-taps-journey-co-creator-robin-hunicke-to-teach-game-development/.

Keiko Erikawa

Kapell, Matthew, and Andrew B. R. Elliott. *Playing with the Past: Digital Games and the
Simulation of History*. Bloomsbury, 2013.

Kim, Hyeshin. "Women's Games in Japan: Gendered Identity and Narrative
    Construction." *Theory, Culture & Society*, vol. 26, no. 2–3, 2009, pp. 165–188, doi:
    10.1177/0263276409103132.

Kotaku. "Gita & Tim Play Angelique (Super Famicom, 1994)." *YouTube* video, 1:08:23,
    January 17, 2018, www.youtube.com/watch?v=lXdUcDBM0s4&ab_channel=Kotaku.

Nakamura, Toshi. "How Japan Began Making Otome Games." *Kotaku*, June 12, 2015, kotaku.com
    /how-japan-began-making-otome-games-1710577005.

"Translation: An Interview with Keiko Erikawa, the Pioneer of Games Marketed Toward Women."
    Karasu Corps, June 26, 2016, karasucorps.wordpress.com/2016/04/09/translation-an
    -interview-with-keiko-erikawa-the-pioneer-of-games-marketed-toward-women/.

Young, Georgina. "The History of Otome and the Ruby Team Legacy." *IGN India*, July 5, 2019,
    in.ign.com/neo-angelique-psp/136977/feature/the-history-of-otome-and-the-ruby
    -team-legacy.

Brenda Laurel

Beato, G. "Girl Games." *Wired*, Conde Nast, April 1, 1997, www.wired.com/1997/04/es-girlgames/.

Beete, Paulette. "Brenda Laurel: Girls Just Wanna . . . Play Video Games," *American Artscape*,
    2018, No. 1, www.arts.gov/stories/magazine/2018/1/women-arts-galvanizing-encouraging
    -inspiring/brenda-laurel.

Kafai, Yasmin, Carrie Heeter, Jill Denner, and Jennifer Sun. *Beyond Barbie and Mortal Kombat:
    New Perspectives on Gender and Gaming*. MIT Press, 2008.

Kocurek, Carly A. *Brenda Laurel: Pioneering Games for Girls*. Bloomsbury Academic
    & Professional, 2017.

Laurel, Brenda. "Brenda Laurel: 'Why Not Make Video Games for Girls?'" TED, 1998,
    www.ted.com/talks/brenda_laurel_why_not_make_video_games_for_girls/transcript?
    language=en.

Laurel, Brenda. *Utopian Entrepreneur*. MIT Press, 2001.

Auriea Harvey

Harvey, Auriea, and Michaël Samyn. *Tale of Tales*, tale-of-tales.com/index.php.

Kumar, Mathew. "IndieCade: Uncharted's Unlikely Indie Inspirations." *Gamasutra*,
    October 7, 2011, www.gamasutra.com/view/news/127538/IndieCade_Uncharteds_Unlikely
    _Indie_Inspirations.php.

"Meet the 2017 No Quarter Artists: Auriea Harvey." *NYU Game Center*, October 16, 2017,
    gamecenter.nyu.edu/meet-2017-no-quarter-artists-auriea-harvey/.

NYU Game Center. "NYU Game Center Lecture Series Presents Auriea Harvey,
    Choosing My Own Adventure." *YouTube* video, 2:07:04, March 5, 2019, www.youtube.com
    /watch?v=mPaVRsj0hqQ&app=desktop&ab_channel=NYUGameCenter.

Suellentrop, Chris. "Saluting the Women Behind the Screen." *The New York Times*,
August 19, 2014, www.nytimes.com/2014/08/20/arts/video-games/those
-underappreciated-female-video-game-pioneers.html.

Amy Hennig

Fritz, Ben. "How I Made It: Amy Hennig." *Los Angeles Times*, February 7, 2010,
www.latimes.com/archives/la-xpm-2010-feb-07-la-fi-himi7-2010feb07-story.html.

McCarthy, Caty. "The Amy Hennig Interview: On What Changed With Uncharted 4,
Leaving EA, and What's Next." *US Gamer*, February 28, 2019, www.usgamer.net/articles
/amy-hennig-interview-uncharted-4-leaving-ea-ragtag-star-wars.

Takahashi, Dean. "Amy Hennig Interview: Surviving the Trauma of Making a Video Game
and Inspiring Newcomers." *VentureBeat*, February 22, 2019, venturebeat.com/2019/02/22
/amy-hennig-interview-surviving-the-trauma-of-making-a-video-game-and-inspiring
-newcomers/view-all/.

Wood, Rachel L. "Uncharted Territory: Female Authorship in the Literary and Video Game
Marketplaces." *Honors College Theses* 23 (2017), https://digitalcommons.murraystate.edu
/honorstheses/23.

Carol Shaw

"Carol Shaw." *Atari Women*, March 13, 2019, www.atariwomen.org/stories/carol-shaw/.

Edwards, Benj. "VC&G Interview: Carol Shaw, Atari's First Female Video Game Developer."
Vintage Computing and Gaming, October 12, 2011, www.vintagecomputing.com/index.php/
archives/800/vcg-interview-carol-shaw-female-video-game-pioneer-2.

Symonds, Shannon. "Preserving Carol Shaw's Trailblazing Video Game Career."
Play Stuff Blog, The Strong National Museum of Play, July 19, 2017, www.museumofplay.org/
blog/chegheads/2017/07/preserving-carol-shaws-trailblazing-video-game-career.

Mabel Addis Mergardt

Fernandez-Vara, Clara. "Play's the Thing: A Framework to Study Videogames as Performance."
2009 DiGRA International Conference: Breaking New Ground: Innovation in Games, Play,
Practice and Theory (September 2009).

Gardner, Jack. "Three Women Who Shaped Modern Gaming." *Extra Life*, March 2, 2020, extralife
.childrensmiraclenetworkhospitals.org/three-women-who-shaped-modern-gaming/.

Henley, Stacey. "Remembering Mabel Addis, the First Video Game Writer, on International
Women's Day," *GamesRadar*, March 8, 2020, www.gamesradar.com/remembering-mabel
-addis-the-first-video-game-writer-on-international-womens-day/.

Lopez de Castilla, Mariana. "History of Educational Games." *Playful Learning*, December 9, 2018,
commons.pratt.edu/playful-learning/history-of-educational-games/.

Symonds, Shannon. "Defining the Female Gamer." *Cultural Analysis*, vol. 16, no. 2, 2017, p. 42.

Willaert, Kate. "The Sumerian Game: The Most Important Video Game You've Never Heard Of."
    A Critical Hit!, September 9, 2019, www.acriticalhit.com/sumerian-game-most-important
    -video-game-youve-never-heard/.

Danielle Bunten Berry

Bunten Berry, Danielle. "Welcome to My Personal Homepage (and Shrine to Narcissism)."
    Danielle's Homepage, web.archive.org/web/20110707145941/http://www.anticlockwise.com
    /dani/personal/index.html.
(Dani Bunten Berry) Papers, 1949–1998. International Center for the History of
    Electronic Games. Strong Museum, Rochester, New York.
Hague, James. *Halcyon Days: Interviews with Classic Computer and Video Game Programmers*.
    www.dadgum.com/halcyon/.
Kim, Ryan. "Dani Bunten Berry, Pioneering Video Game Designer Makes the Hall of Fame."
    SFGate, February 8, 2007, blog.sfgate.com/techchron/2007/02/08/dani-bunten-berry
    -pioneering-video-game-designer-makes-the-hall-of-fame/.
Koon, David. "Dani Bunten Changed Video Games Forever." *Arkansas Times*, February 8, 2012,
    arktimes.com/news/cover-stories/2012/02/08/dani-bunten-changed-video-games-forever.
Meagher-Swanson, L. "In Memorial: A Tribute to Danielle Bunten Berry." *Gamasutra*,
    www.gamasutra.com/blogs/LMeagherSwanson/20120601/171574/In_Memorial_A
    _Tribute_to_Danielle_Bunten_Berry.php.

Corrinne Yu

Bort, Julie. "The 39 Most Powerful Female Engineers of 2018." *Business Insider*, June 21, 2018,
    www.businessinsider.com/the-most-powerful-female-engineers-of-2018-2018-4.
Crecente, Brian. "Halo 4's Former Principal Engineer Is Now Helping with Amazon's
    Drone Fleet." *Polygon*, April 28, 2015, www.polygon.com/2015/4/28/8507543
    /Corrinne-yu-amazon-halo-naughty-dog.
Wozniak, Steve. "Meet Corrinne Yu, the Influential Programmer Who Gave up Nuclear Physics
    for Play." *Edge Magazine*, March 13, 2014, n4g.com/news/1484293/meet-corrinne-yu-the
    -influential-programmer-who-gave-up-nuclear-physics-for-play.

Rebecca Heineman

Barton, Matt. "The Burger Speaks: An Interview With an Archmage." *Gamasutra*,
    December 27, 2010, www.gamasutra.com/view/feature/134614/the_burger_speaks
    _an_interview_.php?print=1.
Barton, Matt. *Honoring the Code: Conversations with Great Game Designers*. CRC Press, 2013.
"Rebecca Heineman, CEO." *Olde Sküül: Play With Us!*, oldeskuul.com/rebecca_bio.php.

Stratis, Niko. "The Secret Trans History of Gaming, According to Rebecca Heineman."
    Xtra Magazine, October 29, 2020, xtramagazine.com/culture/rebecca-heineman
    -trans-high-score-183508.

Amy Briggs

Buck, Stephanie. "In the Boys-Only Market of Early Video Games, Amy Briggs Built
    the First One for Girls." *Timeline*, March 27, 2017, timeline.com/plundered-hearts
    -amy-briggs-7c8699847bed.

deMause, Neil. "Romancing the Genre: An Interview with Plundered Hearts Author Amy Briggs."
    XYZZY News, April 12, 2005, www.xyzzynews.com/xyzzy.12d.html.

Maher, Jimmy. "Plundered Hearts." *The Digital Antiquarian*, October 23, 2015, www.filfre.net
    /2015/10/plundered-hearts/.

Salter, Anastasia. "Plundered Hearts: Infocom, Romance, and the History of Feminist
    Game Design." *Feminist Media Histories*, vol. 6, no. 1, 2020, pp. 66–92, doi: 10.1525/
    fmh.2020.6.1.66.

Yoko Shimomura

"Blending Worlds With Music: Interview With Composer Yoko Shimomura."
    OTAQUEST, December 26, 2019, www.otaquest.com/yoko-shimomura-interview/.

Dwyer, Nick. "Interview: Street Fighter II's Yoko Shimomura." *Red Bull Music Academy Daily*,
    September 18, 2014, daily.redbullmusicacademy.com/2014/09/yoko-shimomura-interview.

Goldner, Sam. "The Composer of Kingdom Hearts Has Never Stopped Reinventing Herself."
    VICE, September 6, 2019, www.vice.com/en/article/pa7gnz/the-composer-of-kingdom
    -hearts-has-never-stopped-reinventing-herself.

Heaney, Duncan. "KINGDOM HEARTS: Yoko Shimomura Talks Dearly Beloved:
    Square Enix Blog." *Square Enix*, December 1, 2020, square-enix-games.com
    /en_GB/news/yoko-shimomura-dearly-beloved.

Jade Raymond

Adkins, John. "The Untold Origins of Gamergate—and the Gaming Legends Who Spawned
    the Modern Culture of Abuse." *Mic*, July 12, 2017, www.mic.com/articles/180888
    /erik-wolpaw-chet-faliszek-old-man-murray-untold-origins-of-gamergate-harassment
    -abuse-gaming-culture.

Crecente, Brian. "20 Years a Developer, Jade Raymond Weighs Her Next Step." *Polygon*,
    February 26, 2015, www.polygon.com/2015/2/26/8078083/jade-raymond-next-step.

Leijon, Erik. "Jade Raymond: Taking Her Game to a Whole New Level." *McGill Alumni*, January
    2020, mcgillnews.mcgill.ca/s/1762/news/interior.aspx?sid=1762&gid=2&pgid=2152.

Potanin, Robin. "Forces in Play." *Fun and Games '10: Proceedings of the 3rd International
    Conference on Fun and Games*, September 2010, pp. 135–143, doi: 10.1145/1823818.1823833.

Takahashi, Dean. "Jade Raymond's Growing Empire at Ubisoft (Interview)."
    VentureBeat, March 31, 2013, venturebeat.com/2013/03/31/jade-raymonds
    -growing-empire-at-ubisoft-interview/.

Joyce Weisbecker

Audureau, William. "Joyce Weisbecker, Pionnière Méconnue De La Programmation De Jeux Vidéo."
    Le Monde.fr, November 9, 2017, www.lemonde.fr/pixels/article/2017/11/09/joyce-weisbecker
    -pionniere-meconnue-de-la-programmation-de-jeux-video_5212437_4408996.html.
"Badass Women in Gaming." *GameSpot*, March 2, 2018, www.gamespot.com/articles
    /badass-women-in-gaming/1100-6457050/.
Gonzalez, Miguel. "Influential Women in Gaming Share Industry Insights." *The Signal*,
    April 24, 2018, tcnjsignal.net/2018/04/24/influential-women-in-gaming-share
    -industry-insights/.
Kartik, Divya. "Joyce Weisbecker." *Game On, Girl*, September 23, 2020, www.gameongirl.co.uk
    /post/design-a-stunning-blog.
McCracken, Harry. "Rediscovering History's Lost First Female Video Game Designer."
    Fast Company, October 27, 2017, www.fastcompany.com/90147592/rediscovering-historys
    -lost-first-female-video-game-designer.

Laura Nikolich

Barnes, Adam. "The History of Spider-Man." *Retro Gamer*, June 13, 2019, www.pressreader.com
    /uk/retro-gamer/20190613/281694026277196.
Campbell, Colin. "The Story of the First Spider-Man Game." *Polygon*, September 14, 2018,
    www.polygon.com/2018/9/14/17856020/spider-man-game-1982-atari-2600-laura
    -nikolich-not-ps4.
"Laura Nikolich." *Atari Women*, May 13, 2019, www.atariwomen.org/stories/laura-nikolich/.
"Spider-Man Plays SPIDER-MAN!" *BLIP The Video Games Magazine*, vol. 1, no. 2,
    Mar. 1983, pp. 2–13.
Stilphen, Scott. "Laura Nikolich Interview." *Atari Compendium*, 2005, https://www.
    ataricompendium.com/archives/interviews/laura_nikolich/interview_laura_nikolich.html.

Brenda Romero

Brophy-Warren, Jamin. "The Board Game No One Wants to Play More Than Once."
    The Wall Street Journal, June 24, 2009, www.wsj.com/articles/BL-SEB-2186.
Campbell, Colin. "Brenda Romero Blasts Game Industry Culture of Blaming Sexual
    Harassment Victims." *Polygon*, March 20, 2014, www.polygon.com/2014/3/20/5530790
    /brenda-romero-game-industry-culture-victim-blaming.

Evans-Thirlwell, Edwin. "Brenda Romero versus the Systems of Pain." *Eurogamer.net*,
July 14, 2017, www.eurogamer.net/articles/2017-05-17-brenda-romero-versus-the
-systems-of-pain.

Parkin, Simon. "How Making Games Helped Her Deal With Evil." *Kotaku*, June 24, 2014,
kotaku.com/brenda-romeros-quest-for-healing-1595394683.

Terdiman, Daniel. "Game Developers Form Sex 'Special Interest Group.'" *CNET*, August 17, 2005,
www.cnet.com/news/game-developers-form-sex-special-interest-group/.

Yao, Mike Z., Chad Mahood, and Daniel Linz. "Sexual Priming, Gender Stereotyping,
and Likelihood to Sexually Harass: Examining the Cognitive Effects of Playing a
Sexually-Explicit Video Game." *Sex Roles*, vol. 62, no. 1–2, 22 Sept. 2009, pp. 77–88, doi:
10.1007/s11199-009-9695-4.

Megan Gaiser

Gaiser, Megan. "Solving the Mystery of the Missing Girl Games." *The Video Game Revolution*, PBS,
www.pbs.org/kcts/videogamerevolution/impact/girl_games.html.

Marie, Meagan. *Women in Gaming: 100 Professionals of Play*. Prima Games, an Imprint of
Random House LLC, 2018.

Sachs, Zoey. "The Un-Barbie of Gaming." *New York Post*, July 12, 2010, nypost.com/2010/07/12
/the-un-barbie-of-gaming/.

Jane Jensen

Andreadis, Kosta. "Revisiting Gabriel Knight: Sins of the Fathers." *IGN*, September 8, 2014,
www.ign.com/articles/2014/09/08/revisiting-gabriel-knight-sins-of-the-fathers?page=1.

Hernández-Pérez, Manuel. "Jane Jensen: Gabriel Knight, Adventure Games, Hidden Objects."
Journal of Gender Studies, vol. 28, no. 4, 2019, pp. 492–494, doi: 10.5040/9781501327445.

Jensen, Jane. "r/IAmA—I'm Jane Jensen, Game Designer and Author. AMA!" *Reddit*,
October 9, 2014, www.reddit.com/r/IAmA/comments/2irxex/im_jane_jensen
_game_designer_and_author_ama/.

Salter, Anastasia. *Jane Jensen: Gabriel Knight, Adventure Games, Hidden Objects*. Bloomsbury
Academic, an Imprint of Bloomsbury Publishing Inc., 2017.

Wallis, Alistair. "Playing Catch Up: Gabriel Knight's Jane Jensen." *Gamasutra*, May 17, 2007,
www.gamasutra.com/view/news/104930/Playing_Catch_Up_Gabriel_Knights_Jane_Jensen.php.

"Women's History Month: Jane Jensen, Creator of Gabriel Knight." *IGDA WIG SIG*, March 5, 2019,
women.igda.org/2019/03/05/womens-history-month-jane-jensen-creator-of-gabriel-knight/.

Linda Currie

Aihoshi, Richard. "Linda and Ian Currie Interview." *IGN*, June 20, 2012, www.ign.com
/articles/2003/01/10/linda-and-ian-currie-interview.

Kazemi, Darius. *Jagged Alliance 2: Boss Fight Books #5*. Boss Fight Books, 2014.

Newnham, Danielle. *Female Innovators at Work: Women on Top of Tech.* Apress, 2016.

Ruberg, Bonnie. "Women in Games: The Gamasutra 20." *Gamasutra*, May 21, 2008,
www.gamasutra.com/view/feature/131993/women_in_games_the_gamasutra_20.php?page=4.

Sheri Graner Ray

Ray, Sheri Graner. *Gender Inclusive Game Design: Expanding The Market.* Cengage Learning, 2003.

Thiegs, Lisa. "Level Up." St. Edwards University, 2020, www.stedwards.edu/articles
/featured-stories/2020/04/level.

"We've Been Here from the Beginning: WIG SIG Profiles Designer Sheri Graner Ray."
IGDA WIG SIG, June 8, 2018, women.igda.org/2018/06/07/weve-been-here-from-the
-beginning-wig-sig-profiles-designer-sheri-graner-ray/.

Elonka Dunin

Batz, Jeannette. "When Dragons Escape." *Riverfront Times*, June 19, 2002,
www.riverfronttimes.com/stlouis/when-dragons-escape/Content?oid=2468031.

Daniels, Nicole. "Lesson of the Day: 'This Sculpture Holds a Decades-Old C.I.A. Mystery.
And Now, Another Clue.'" *The New York Times*, April 6, 2020, www.nytimes.com
/2020/04/06/learning/kryptos-code-lesson.html.

Donlan, Christian. "The Game Developer, the CIA, and the Sculpture Driving Them Crazy."
Eurogamer.net, October 6, 2014, www.eurogamer.net/articles/2014-06-08-the-game
-developer-the-cia-and-the-sculpture-driving-them-crazy.

Dunin, Elonka. "Elonka Dunin" Autobiography, April 24, 2011, elonka.com/autobiography.html.

Dunin, Elonka. "r/IAmA—Hi, I Am Elonka Dunin. Cryptographer, GameDev, Namesake for
Dan Brown's 'Nola Kaye' Character, and Maintainer of a List of the World's Most Famous
Unsolved Codes, Including One at the Center of CIA Headquarters, the Encrypted Kryptos
Sculpture. Ask Me Anything!" *Reddit*, July 9, 2019, www.reddit.com/r/IAmA/comments
/cb95qa/hi_i_am_elonka_dunin_cryptographer_gamedev/.

Dunin, Elonka, and Klaus Schmeh. *Codebreaking: A Practical Guide.* Little, Brown
Book Group, 2020.

Hinge, Mark, and Peter Prickett. "Interview: Elonka Dunin." *Whitedust*, March 14, 2006,
elonka.com/mirrors/whitedust/interview.html.

Linebaugh, Mack. "A Nashville Cryptography Expert Has Been Trying To Crack This CIA
Riddle For 16 Years." *WPLN News—Nashville Public Radio*, September 9, 2016, wpln.org/post
/a-nashville-cryptography-expert-has-been-trying-to-crack-this-cia-riddle-for-16-years/.

ACKNOWLEDGMENTS

THERE ARE TOO MANY PEOPLE TO THANK, BUT I'M GONNA TRY.

THIS BOOK WOULDN'T exist without Eric Smith, my literary agent and a wonderful advocate for authors, gamers, and geeks everywhere. Thank you for taking a chance on me and for your constant work to make sure there's room for everyone at the table.

I couldn't have written this book without Britny Brooks-Perilli, Amber Morris, and the teams at Running Press and P.S. Literary. Your insights and feedback challenged me in all the right ways and made this a book to be proud of, and I'm so happy we could put it into the world.

Thank you to everyone at the NYU Game Center. Games 101 was the seed that grew into this book: thank you for introducing me to this history. In particular, thank you to Clara Fernandez-Vara and Naomi Clark. Your thoughtfulness, advocacy, and passion for games, criticism, and pop culture inspire me every day. This book truly wouldn't exist without you.

My eternal thanks go to Jess Erion, who worked tirelessly to fact-check, gut-check, and add additional thoughts and commentary on this book. Reading through your notes kept me thinking and laughing through many long nights. Also a huge thanks to my friends and readers, Clara, Lisa Hunter, and Alex Epstein.

My admiration and thanks will be with all of the women profiled in this book, who did so much to inspire the generations that came after them. You and your work have made me a better creator and more thoughtful person. In particular, I'd like to thank all of the women who took the time to talk with me: Dona Bailey, Megan Gaiser, Brenda Laurel, Brenda Romero, Sheri Graner Ray, Elonka Dunin, Joyce Weisbecker, Rebecca Heineman, and Jane Jensen. Getting to talk to you was a dream come true.

So many thanks go to my coworkers at Insomniac Games, all of whom were so supportive of this book. Making games with you has been a highlight in my career and life, and I'm proud of the positive impact we're having on the world.

My friends and family supported me through every step of writing this book: from offering me a lakeside cabin to write in to urging me to take a break with a well-placed *Dungeons & Dragons* session. Thank you in particular to Taylor Cyr, David Frisch, Dan Kimsey, Jordan Emily, Taryn Malher, Sarah Hann, and Lauren Mee, who all listened to me gush about the "fun facts" I was learning—for *years*.

Thank you to my mom, Laurie Girardot, who loved to hear all the updates about the book and who, as a single mom, raised me with the confidence to believe I deserved a seat at the table.

And thank you, finally, to my husband, Jason Allen. From the moment I told you, "I think I'm writing a book? Maybe?" you were supportive in every way imaginable, and then some. You knew when to push me to keep going and when to urge me to take breaks, and you never let me give up on myself. Thank you, and I love you.